D0927045

The
PROJECTIVE USE
of the
BENDER GESTALT

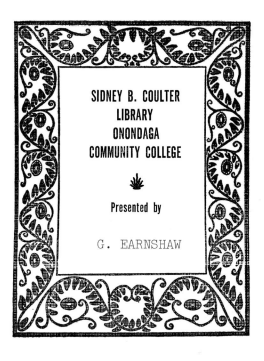

Publication Number 854

AMERICAN LECTURE SERIES®

A Monograph in

AMERICAN LECTURES IN PSYCHOLOGY

Edited by

MOLLY HARROWER, Ph.D.

Professor of Psychology
University of Florida
Gainesville, Florida

The
PROJECTIVE USE
of the
BENDER GESTALT

By

EDNA ALBERS LERNER

Clinical Assistant Professor
of Psychology in Psychiatry
Cornell University Medical College
Assistant Attending Psychologist of
The New York Hospital—(Payne Whitney Clinic)

CHARLES C THOMAS · PUBLISHER

Springfield · Illinois · U.S.A.

Published and Distributed Throughout the World by

CHARLES C THOMAS • PUBLISHER

Bannerstone House

301-327 East Lawrence Avenue, Springfield, Illinois, U.S.A.

© *1972, by* CHARLES C. THOMAS • PUBLISHER

ISBN 0-398-02495-2 (Cloth)

ISBN 0-398-02496-0 (Paper)

Library of Congress Catalog Card Number: 71-190329

With THOMAS BOOKS *careful attention is given to all details of
manufacturing and design. It is the Publisher's desire to present books
that are satisfactory as to their physical qualities and artistic possibilities
and appropriate for their particular use.* THOMAS BOOKS *will be true
to those laws of quality that assure a good name and good will.*

Printed in the United States of America

C-1

INTRODUCTION

THIS is a brief handbook on the use of the Bender Gestalt as a tool for students and practitioners of projective testing. It departs from the historical application of the test as presented and evolved by Lauretta Bender in her research on developmental factors, organicity, and regression. This material is empirically derived from experience with the test over a decade, in hospital and clinic settings, in schools and private practice. I use it as one of a battery of projective tests, but to my mind it has a special place as a fairly quick instrument for a preliminary assessment.

The literature on the projective significance of the Bender is scanty compared to that of the Rorschach, though mimeographed notes, especially those of Dr. Fred Brown, have been in circulation for some years. I have not intended this presentation as exhaustive, or backed by statistical studies, but as one way of looking at the Bender product. The range and variety of the illustrative material presented here conveys better than words what this particular test can contribute.

In discussing the basic figures and the variations upon them I have tried to avoid the simplistic or dogmatic and to stress options of interpretation that are open, and that contribute to insight. But I have not hesitated to offer my own interpretations. At this stage, as the projective approach gains acceptance, it is only the pooling of hypotheses and insights from various sources, and from practitioners with different patient populations and frames of reference, that can benefit us all.

While my interpretations and conclusions are my own, I want specifically to thank Dr. Fred Brown, Chairman of the Department of Psychology of Mount Sinai Hospital, for introducing me to the projective approach to the Bender and for his innovative and stimulating presentation of this point of view. Thanks are also expressed to Dr. Sanford Goldstone, Dr. David Clayson, and Dr. Elizabeth Welker, colleagues at the Payne Whitney Clinic for generously sharing their patients' productions; and to Miss Myrtle Guy and Mrs. Katie Hicks for their assistance in organizing the material.

EDNA ALBERS LERNER

CONTENTS

All figures and cards have been reduced to
75 percent of their original size.

The
PROJECTIVE USE
of the
BENDER GESTALT

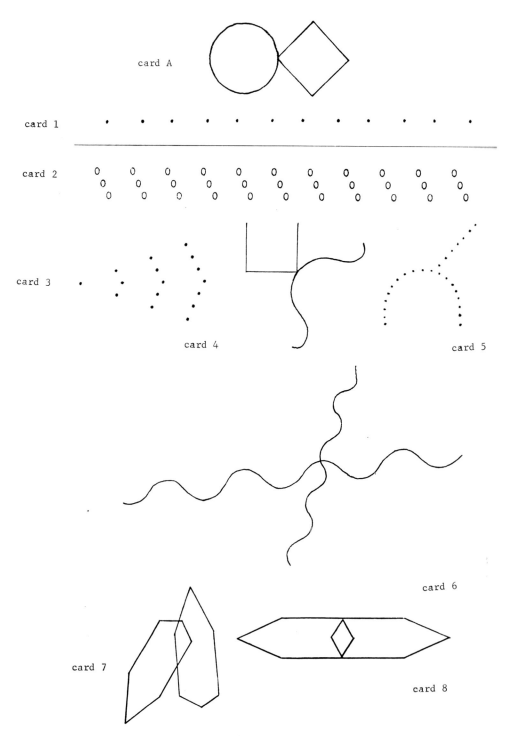

Figure 1.

Chapter I

APPROACHES TO THE TEST AS A WHOLE

THE Bender Visual Motor Gestalt Test was evolved by Lauretta Bender from Max Wertheimer's studies of gestalt principles governing perception, and was used as an index of developmental level, to measure intellectual efficiency and to explore organic impairment. This was later broadened to include the study of personality, with special reference to regression. The projective emphasis has increased in recent years, initiated and supported by Dr. Fred Brown and Dr. Max L. Hutt. It is with this last development that the present study is concerned.

The assumption is that the Bender may be used in the manner of a simplified, linear Rorschach. Since chromatic color and shading are absent, we miss much that is elicited by the richer Rorschach material. The viewer is confined to form, to the single figure or combined figures with which he is presented, but he does more than simply take them in passively. "All perception is apperception" as the gestaltists say, and in the process of "seeing," clusters of associations appear to crystallize for the viewer; a symbolic process is initiated which sets the theme to which each person responds uniquely. He then projects on the figures the attitudes, anxieties, wishes, and fears which have been triggered for him. And he communicates these emphases by the way he copies the figures and by how and what he recalls of them.

To start with, the Bender—like the Rorschach—is a flexible, multi-faceted instrument in which no single fact has universal significance, and in which we must always bear in mind the interrelationship of all the parts to each other, and of each to the whole. It is a neutral instrument, and like all good projective tests it can profitably be used within a variety of frameworks.

The test as standardized by Lauretta Bender, consists of nine cards with one figure on each card. The administration preferred by this examiner is first to describe what the test will be: "I am going to give you some patterns to copy. There are nine of them." This deliberate statement of the number of cards to be presented makes the terms of the task explicit. Some examiners feel that it is better to leave the number vague in order to see how the subject adjusts to the challenge of coping with the unknown. In my opinion, the variety of the designs is a sufficient variable for this purpose and I like the opportunity to see how, given a defined problem, a patient plans ahead and, as circumstances change, alters his plan to meet them. After the patient has copied the nine designs, I take his paper away, give him a new sheet and say "Now let me see how many of the designs you can remember."

After the introduction I note the manner of reception of the defined task, and the way in which the patient proceeds to organize for its execution. From the beginning qualitative differences make themselves felt. Some patients are passive and unresisting—and the question arises whether their psychic energies are so involved in other problems that this task seems peripheral and unimportant. Others are hostile and aggressive. They may express their hostility passively by "dribbling" with their pencils, or by a refusal to try, or actively by slashing, cutting productions, by angry scribbling. Some communicate their anxiety by their damp hands and dripping brows. Others attempt indifference—by refusing to steady the sheet with one hand as they casually scrawl with the other. Still others throw up a smoke screen of verbal indifference, a patter of irrelevant comments, even as they surreptitiously strain to compete. And each one begins to provide cues to the unique patterning and color of his particular personality from the first postural or verbal as well as motor response.

The verbal and nonverbal responses to the instructions reflect what the patient is experiencing, and from this may be inferred the patient's characteristic reaction to new situations, to being tested, to adapting to conditions set from without. For example, a schizophrenic patient may demonstrate immediately his poor judgment and lack of boundaries by an expansive outsize version of Card A placed squarely in the middle of the paper. It is as if he could respond only to the initial stimulus—as if anticipation (there are 8 more figures coming), and reality testing (they must all fit on this card) were suspended. What the patient does as he copies subsequent figures offers additional clues, and major and minor deviations from the copy alert us to their special significance.

But the meat of the Bender contribution, from the point of view of projection, lies in the recall, which is administered without warning. In this recall phase the number of figures remembered, which of them are remembered and which forgotten, the order, placement and change of the figures—simplification, elaboration or any distortion—offer a rich variety of projective clues. We note general stylistic considerations of roundness, angularity, pencil pressure and line, flow or jerkiness, need for props, size consistency, sloppiness or fuzziness of delineation, connectedness or fragmentation, reaction and interaction with the examiner, and finally that subtle, not easily defined, quality of style. For perfection, the photographic copy is not necessarily the "best" Bender. What one hopes for is rather a good, but subtly enlivened performance, with well-preserved gestalt, infused with dash and spirit, which has more to offer than a sterile reproduction.

These general considerations provide the frame within which the execution of the single figure, and the relationship or contrast between

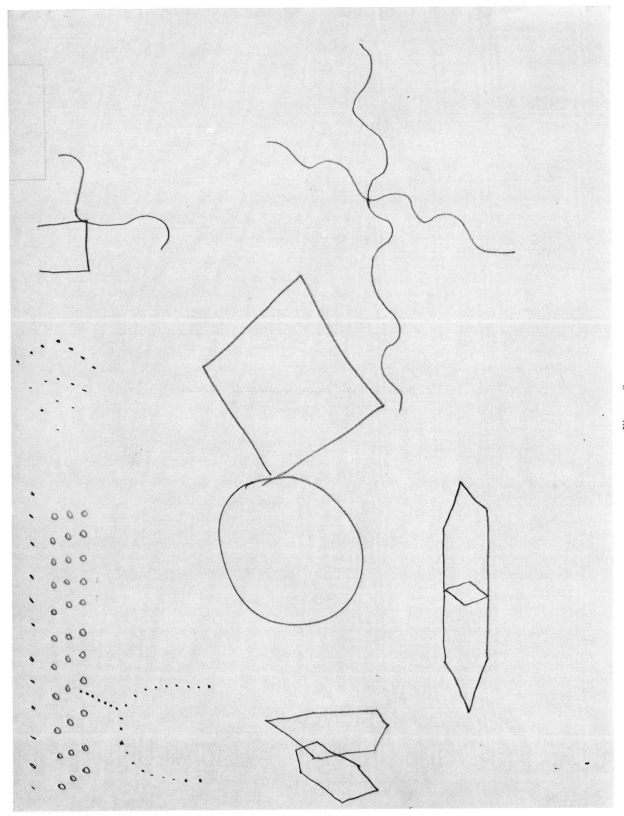

Figure 2.

groups of figures, occur. For the deviations represent an intrusion on reality (as represented by the figure)—an idiosyncratic distortion of memory trace. So it is *that* figure and *that* distortion of the figure to which we must attend. In other words we note what interrupts the presented gestalt, particularly when it is not just a return to a simplified form—though here too we note where the regression occurs. But it is of greater importance when it presents a change, a combination, a rejection of what is given either in the whole figure or in the relationship of the parts, and a shift to a new and altered configuration. Thus many aspects of the Bender are overdetermined—a complicating and enriching fact. And the significance of any one figure depends on how it is related to all the others—what waves and contaminations or simple consistencies are set up—which help to build into and illuminate a psychological whole.

For example, what is the patient's handling of the blank sheet presented him? What does it stand for? How does he conceive it, consciously and unconsciously? How does he cope with the problem it presents? In the simplest terms the blank sheet has defined boundaries. It is the ground on which the figures are to be set. And since the task assigned has to be performed within the limits of those boundaries, how it is performed is characteristic of the patient's coping pattern.

Some patients ignore the boundary aspect: they may make miniscule figures—smaller than the figure presented, tightly grouped, shrinking the field to compassable territory. Some cling, for safety, to the boundary of the sheet (Fig. 12). Some draw outsize expansive figures (Fig. 42a2). Others will draw one huge figure and ask for more paper. And still others will overlay, putting one figure on top of another, ignoring not only the "terms" of the sheet of paper, but the individual boundaries implicit in the fact of the separateness of figures within the series (Fig. 4).

A number of tentative hypotheses and conclusions may be drawn from these facts. The blank paper may be seen as the life space, or as representing reality demands and limitations, as setting the terms of the environment. These defined boundaries evoke ego functions which reflect reality testing, judgment, boundary awareness and respect. Or, more reductively, they reflect cognitive capacities: the ability to anticipate, organize, plan for and execute a task under the terms set—the capacity to demonstrate goal-oriented activity and all that implies.

The impression derived from the initial approach may be positive or negative, or it may be inconclusive. Most people, warned that nine figures will be presented, will start at the top and proceed by some rational scheme to copy the figures in order of presentation. Many

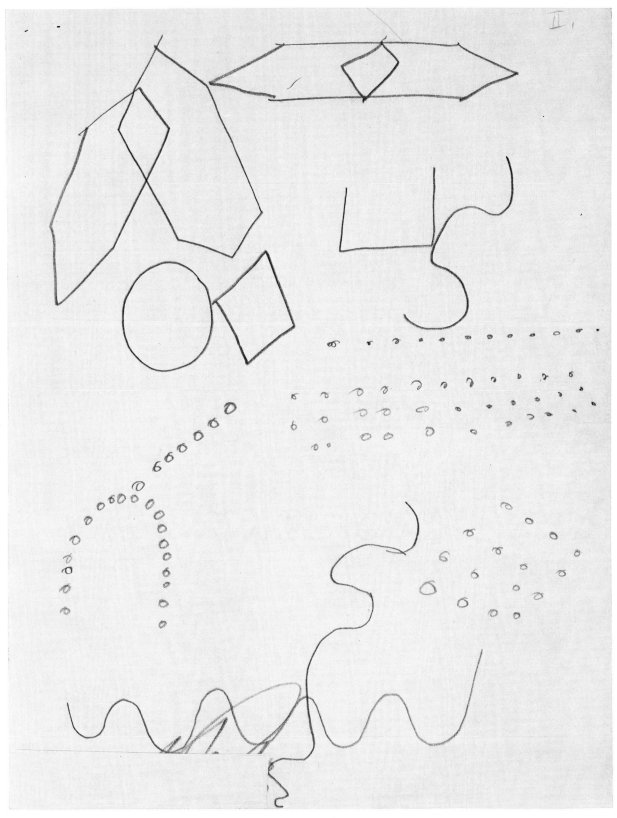

Figure 3.

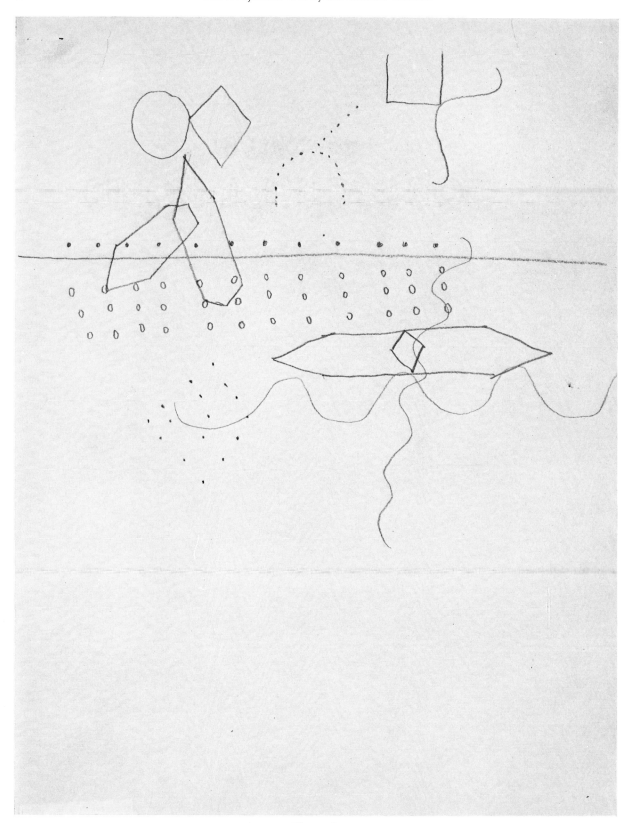

Figure 4.

simply copy them in sequence vertically and, if their productions are large, ask (or do not ask) permission to turn the paper over and continue on the back. Others work horizontally in rows. Still others start out in a systematic way and then digress: one might ask whether it is because a particular figure sets off unconscious reverberations that upset the initial rational plan, or whether it is a positive asset that enables the patient to adapt flexibly to the requirements of each figure and the shifting "ground" that the ongoing sequence of figures offers.

This response may conceivably reflect an aesthetic gift, enabling the patient to approach even this simple task creatively, and so organize the figures as to satisfy requirements of logic, figure-ground relationships, and spatial considerations, thus achieving a kind of balanced individualized beauty. A variant of this is presented by the patients who interpret the test wholly as an aesthetic problem. They see the chance to show their capacity for organizing these disparate patterns into a pleasing whole, sometimes interjecting these considerations inappropriately and communicating their preoccupation by pleased comments on the total effect as they work (Fig. 5). This ordered disorder is quite different from a rejection of order or disregard for it.

The manner in which the material is arranged, as well as the fact of organization or disorganization, is also important. Many patients number their figures (which is initially confusing since the Bender Figure "A" inevitably becomes "I"). The numbering may reflect a simple compulsivity, or an effort to control a wild impulsivity, as the contrast between the numbers and the style of Figure 6 suggest. Some draw lines between the figures demonstrating an isolating defense, as well as the compulsivity all rigid arrangements suggest. And others draw boxes (Fig. 7) sometimes in such a manner as to condemn themselves to fit into the box whatever figure is presented, regardless of size or shape. This implies not only rigidity but a respect for rules and order so strong as to be self-defeating—an emphasis on controlling or constricting, on form rather than on content.

This kind of isolating is overrigid; it is a defense that no longer offers leeway for adaptations. But it is very different from the decompensating obsessive-compulsive whose apparent order masks a basic confusion (Fig. 6), and also different from the compensated, even paranoid, patient. He may impose an irrelevant order by setting up irrational groupings, scatter his figures haphazardly and then draw compartments around them, as if not order but decontamination were the problem (see Fig. 51).

These observations on order do not reflect approval of one organizing principle as opposed to another, for a certain adaptive flexibility is perhaps to be preferred to any stereotyped plan. But flagrant

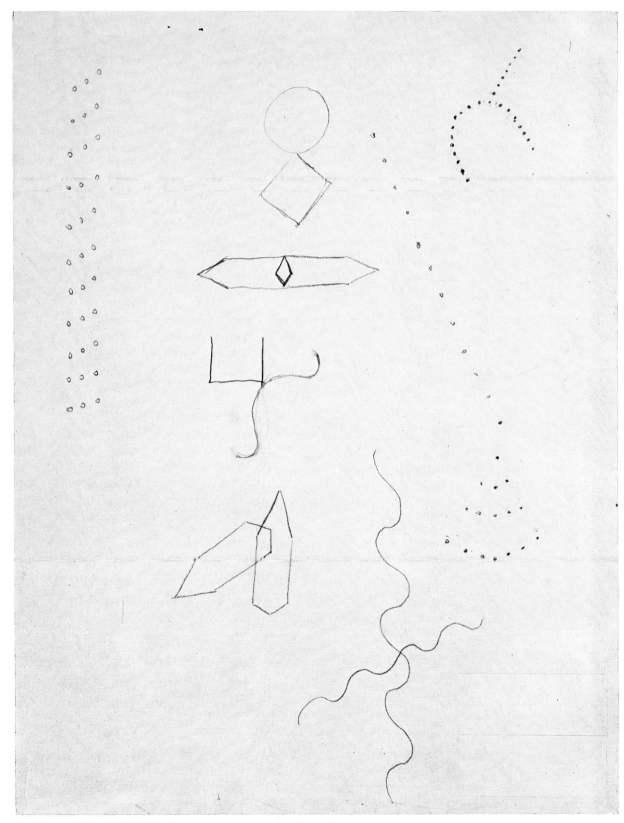

Figure 5.

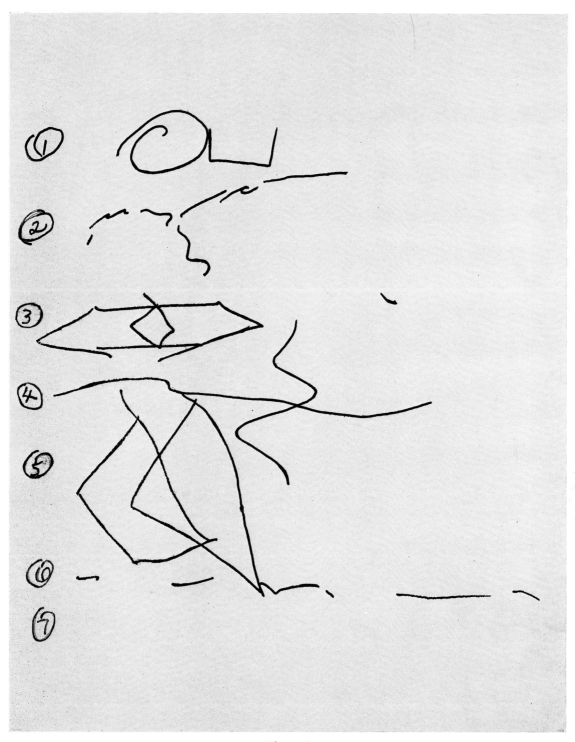

Figure 6.

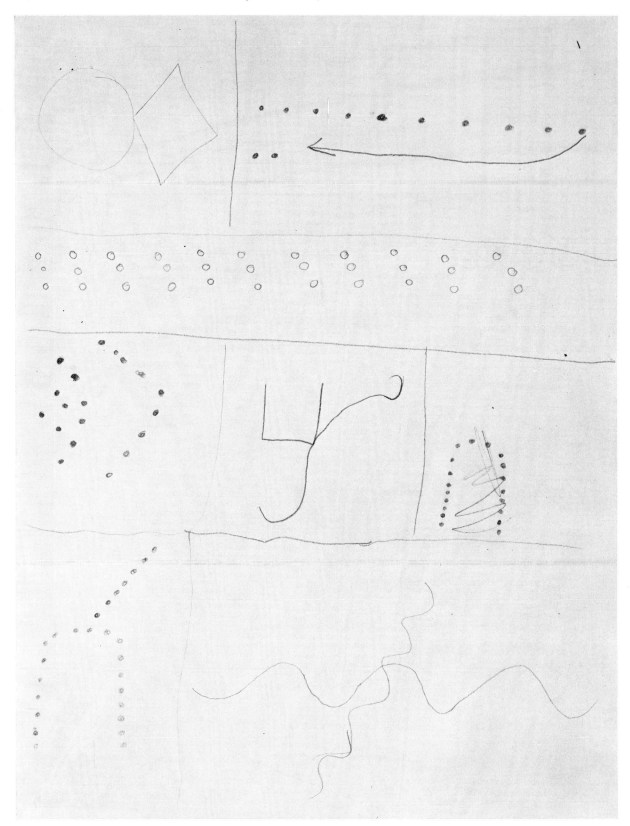

Figure 7.

disorder may communicate pathology dramatically. The hostile aggressive performance of a patient who splashes out a series of responses in random configurations communicates his hostility both to the task and to the examiner, and often he communicates an intensity of aggression easily tapped and poorly controlled (Fig. 6). But the patient who turns his paper randomly, who produces a collection of figures with no edge of the paper consistently up, communicates his own indifference to planning and lack of basic orientation as well (Fig. 8). And a patient who starts out bravely in the middle of the page and then proceeds, condemning himself to more and more difficult problems of fitting is certainly lacking in judgment and foresight. The general organization then, or lack of it; the total figure-ground treatment; the sense of spatial relations with consideration for the individual properties of each figure: these lead to related but different questions.

For example, that of size. Are the figures expansive, compressed, cramped, or miniscule? Some patients, once the scale is set, adhere to it. Or else they introduce variations that correspond to the variations in space requirements of the figures presented to copy. Others force the figures to cohere to some inner standard of their own. These are the people who refuse to accept the task as set and must alter it, subtly or flagrantly, so that they impose their own terms on the performance. We must distinguish between the patient who rigidly standardizes his material according to consistent overall inner rule—that is to say, who prefers to restructure, to take charge, to stay in control even when it is not appropriate, and the patient who suddenly expands a particular figure in response to the touching off of some vulnerable inner chord.

Aside from size, it is important to note the spacing of the figures. They may be almost isolated by space, if not by the more rigid containing devices previously described. Or one figure may be isolated, giving it special significance. Or the figures may clash, collide, sharply and aggressively, or subtly intrude and penetrate. Here we note which ones collide or penetrate (Fig. 9). These aspects communicate not simply aggressivity and inability to control, but the open disregard, intolerance, or indifference toward boundaries—one's own or others.

The problem of consistency, touched on above, is not confined to size or order. One may detect an unevenness of psychic flow, regular swings, or chaotic upsurges in response to particular figures which trigger particular anxieties, and which result in figures markedly inferior (or superior) to the others. Or the figures may group themselves, with all figures involving relationship, or curves, or angles, on a similar level, thus drawing attention to a category of problems.

It is useful to note also, in the recall, not only which figures or cate-

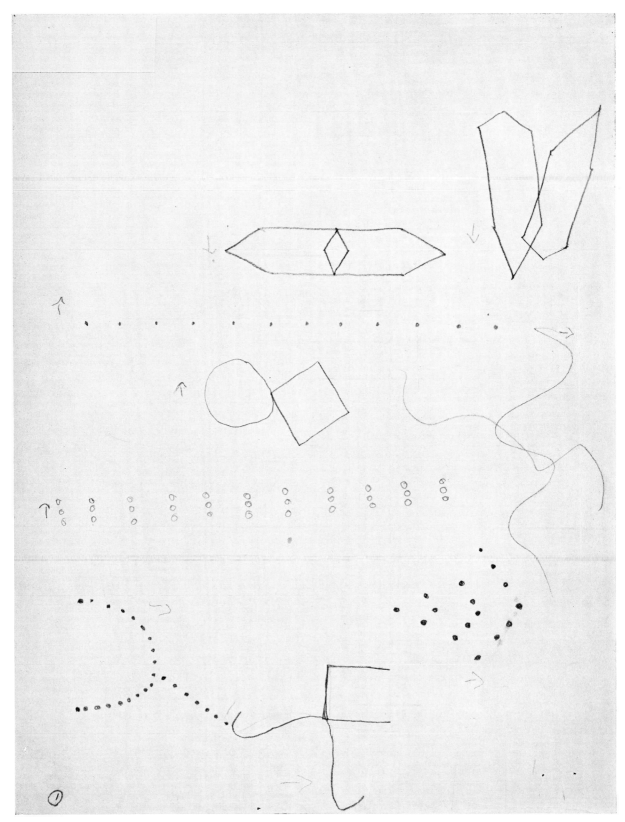

Figure 8.

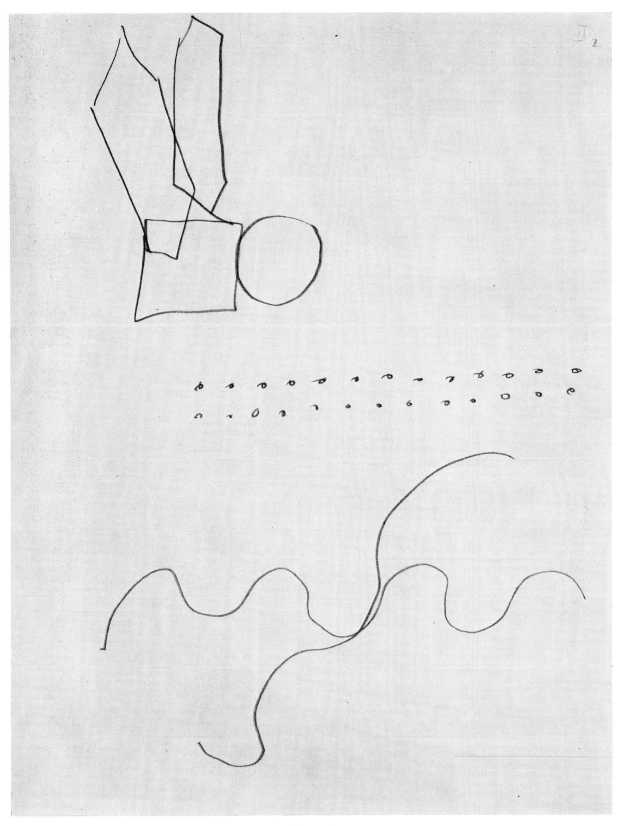

Figure 9.

gories of figures are remembered, but which ones are forgotten. Also what groupings are omitted, what springs first to the mind, what emerges painfully, with effort, or what cannot be forced into consciousness—or, if forced into consciousness, what confabulations (that is new combinations of elements of separate figures) between figures result.

In the recall we observe which figures are dropped, which repressed, and which distorted. The distortions, additions, deletions and combinations may be dramatic, and always underline a significant point. The discussion which follows, on points to look for in the individual figures, particular deviations—some frequent almost popular changes, others unusual—can never hope to cover all the possible variations. The unique performance remains unique, and is what holds continuing interest.

In considering the individual figures several general points are worth keeping in mind. One is the general proposition that curves denote the feminine, and angles the masculine. A second is that the juxtaposition of any two figures evokes, whether consciously or unconsciously, directly or remotely, certain associations to interaction. I am speaking of the basic interactions of man and woman, parent and child, and all the variations superimposed upon them.

A third general point is that many figures, particularly the symmetrical ones, appear to represent on some level a body image. This means that the usual inferences made from figure drawings are relevant here, with the top of the figure representing the rational, cognitive, conscious aspect, and the lower part the body, the instinctual or the unconscious. Up/down axes have other significance too—significances of mood, of aspiration, guilt, shame, failure. And the left/right axis evokes the unconscious/conscious continuum, the left turning inward in fantasy or backward regressively, the right forward, emergent, toward the environment.

None of these inferences are necessarily valid in any particular case, and in any event categories tend to fuse, elide, overlap. Also, as in the Rorschach, figures which usually evoke one set of associations (as for example, the parent-child dependency relationships of the leaning figures in Card 7) may move into another constellation (for example, homosexuality) whose significance emerges from its relationship to other figures in the series or other tests in the battery.

Chapter 2

THE SYMBOLIC PULL OF THE BENDER CARDS

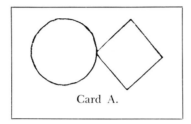

Card A.

CARD A

EXPERIENCE with the Bender cards over time teaches us what basic associations each tends to evoke. As in the Rorschach, we come to expect—or rather to use as a frame of reference—the "popular" symbolic reaction to the card. Some cards have a more explicit "pull" than others, and the first card is among these. Card A, with its touching circle and square, is a basic, archetypal card. It may offer at once a prognostic hint, a characterological impression, and a foretaste of what the other cards will elaborate. It starkly presents the subject with all the decisions we have discussed before: From the way he handles his first card one gets hints of how he will interpret the task, what strictures and limitations he will set for himself, what freedom he will allow himself. How (one asks) will he *place* this first figure? And what cluster of psychic reverberations will it set off?

To begin with, the design is composed of two separate but equal figures with polar, symbolically significant, shapes—the circle and the square. The left, the circle, represents the feminine, the right, the square—the masculine. The way the patient first copies, then recalls this figure tells us how the patient experiences this polarity and relationship. What are the respective sizes of the figures (Figs. 10, 17): who dominates whom? How well can he duplicate them: what of the roundness of the circle, the squareness of the diamond? Are both or only one distorted? Does the circle overlap, not close, become elliptical or lopsided? Is the square elongated, with exaggerated angles, reinforced sides, open or sharpened corners?

The significance of the distortion for the individual varies somewhat with his sex, yet both may view women as overpowering, dominating, or basically flawed. To be unable to draw the sharp angle of the square, or to need to bind the angle by crossed extensions, suggests instinctual problems for the male: an inability to *be* masculine without anxiety, or a need to control and bind the aggressive thrust.

17

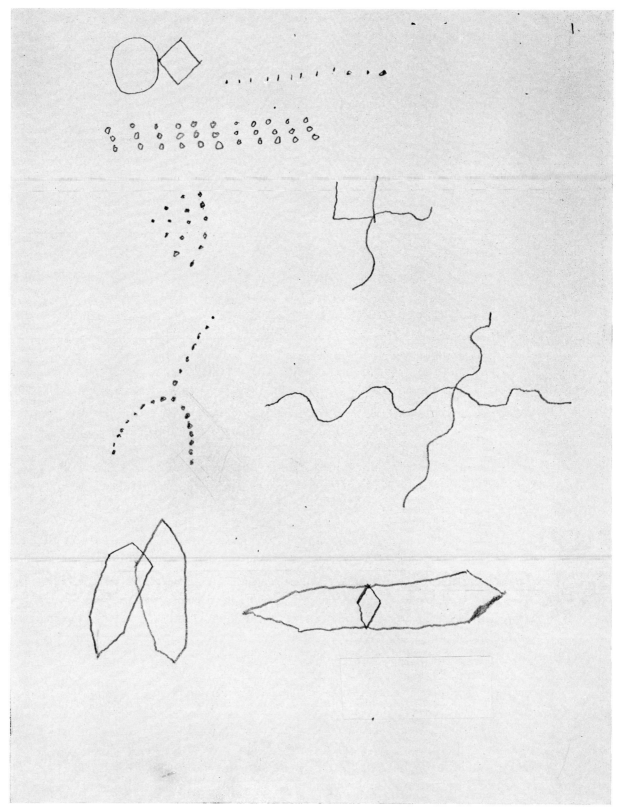

Figure 10.

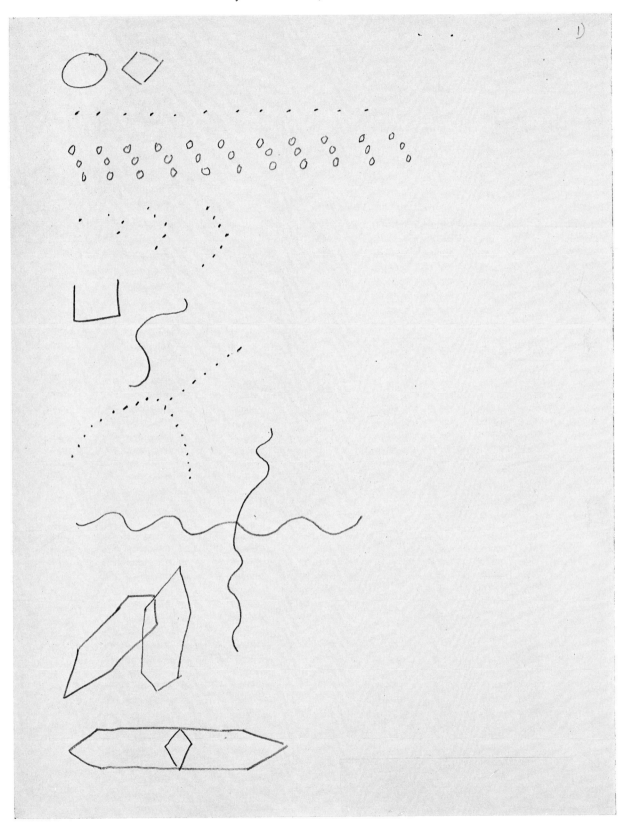

Figure 11.

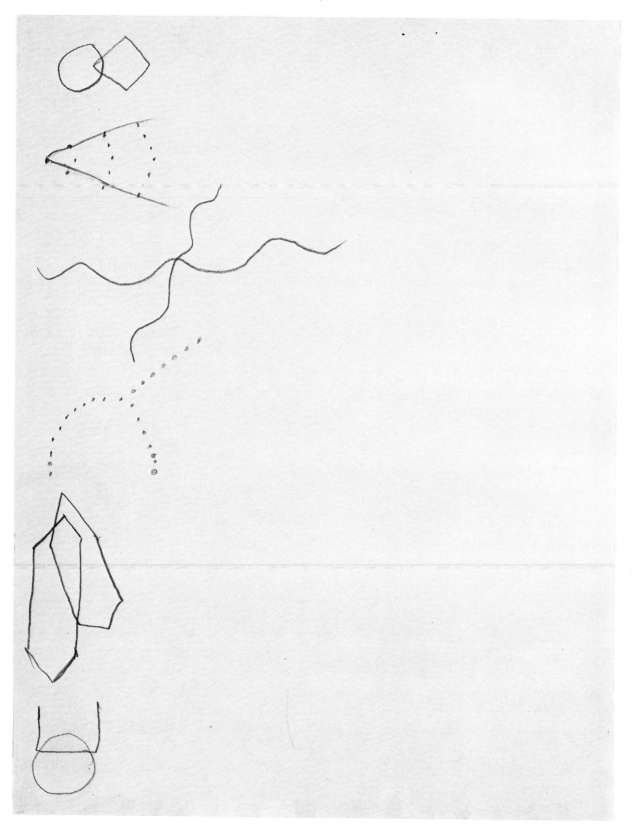

Figure 12.

For a woman, it may express a negative estimate of masculinity, a disappointment about it, or denigration of it.

The double figure also poses in a broad sense the question of all interpersonal relationships, and we note how the figures juxtapose. The optimum is an easy, natural coming together. But this contact may present a problem so threatening and anxiety-provoking that the patient must deliberately try to achieve contact by extension or reinforcement, or by subtle distortions to effect the connection. Or the subject may solve it by leaving a space between the two figures (Fig. 11), in effect by *not* relating, or by jamming them together so that one penetrates the other (Fig. 12). Note that on this recall the hurtful penetration of the feminine by the masculine is later denied (in the bottom version of the figure) by the more subtle rising of the feminine through the masculine—an overpowering and eclipsing of the masculine by the feminine.

When separation or overpenetration occurs, it is of interest to note whether this is the characteristic style of the individual in all juxtaposed figures, or whether it varies from figure to figure depending on which relationships the figures evoke. Does it occur only in connection with particular kinds of relationships: the "heterosexual" figures? the "dependency" figures? Distortion on the first Bender Figure A will immediately alert the examiner to the later connected figures. If an easy natural touch is not achieved, what is his tendency? The kind of connection the patient presents reflects his kind of relating, which either fails to come to terms with the other or goes too far and asks too much, or is easy and adaptive.

Distortions of recall—even of performance—are extremely common on Card A, and the variations on this simple theme are endless. A common distortion is the buffering of male-female contact. Since the relationship is experienced as too threatening, the patient resolves it by shifting the square so that penetration is avoided but a relationship maintained (Fig. 13). Or the relationship may be so fearsome that there is a turning toward the same sex object (Fig. 14).

Another common distortion is to change the relative positions of the figures. On the recall the female may become ascendant—or the male (Fig. 15). Or (a variation), the need to dominate may result in the shift in relative position on the copy: for example, the dominant male on the copy may, on the recall, peel away to reveal the fear of the feminine beneath. Or the feared feminine may be replaced by the male. This sequence analysis between copy and recall can also shed light on questions of characteristic defenses. Does the patient initially perform well, that is faithfully reproduce reality in the copy, and then as the defense collapses, reveal the anxiety producing conflict beneath? Or does he initially pull back, do badly, and on the recall come to terms with his anxieties?

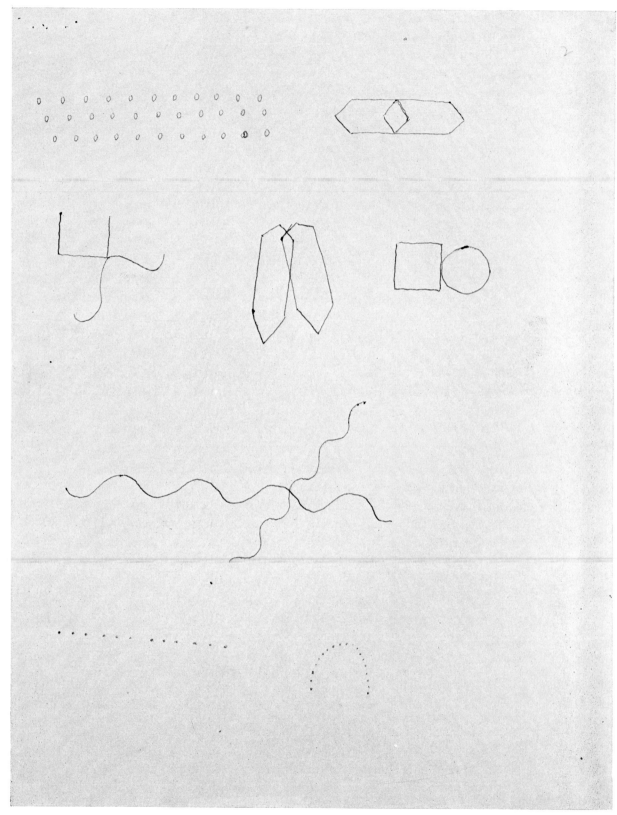

Figure 13.

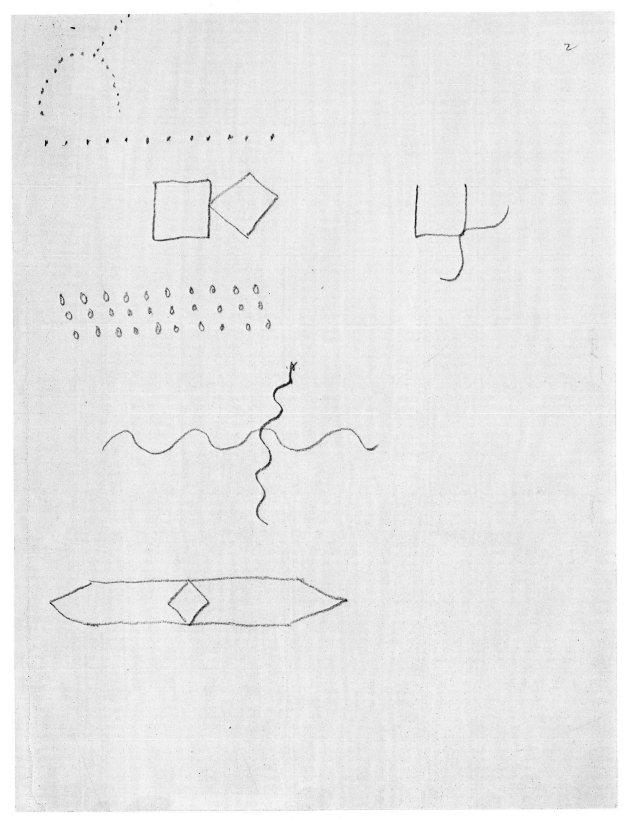

Figure 14.

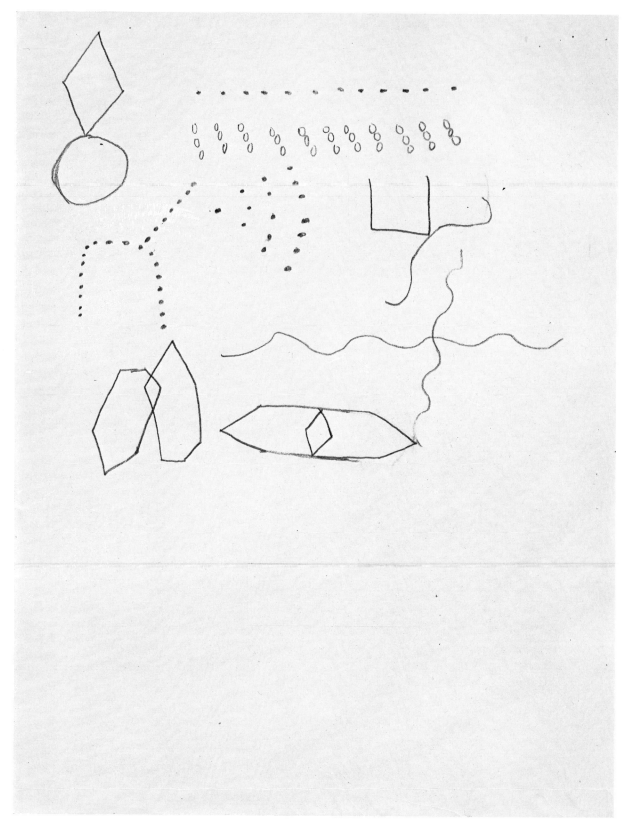

Figure 15.

Card 1.

CARD I

Card 1 is a series of dots in a straight line, subtly grouped in pairs. The problem it presents is a simple one, and marked distortions on this card are less frequent than on many others. The points to be noted in the performance are the tension or equanimity with which the patient accepts the task and sets himself to perform it—reflecting the degree of his basic self-confidence and ability to take the job at face value. If he hesitates, *why* does he hesitate? It may be that any task is too much for him, reflecting poor self-esteem and the habit of failure. Or he may be so incapacitated by anxiety that even this simple visual motor problem is too difficult. Or he may be suspicious of what the significance of the task is. Possibly he is so preoccupied with inner conflicts, or so withdrawn, that to take in and register the task is in itself overwhelming.

Once attempted, we note the size of the figure. It may be tiny and compressed, indicating depression and a lack of psychic energy, or the overcontrol of the extreme compulsive. Or it may spread across the page, sometimes involving two lines to complete the sequence instead of the one presented, almost as if the patient had interpreted the assigned task as "Draw eleven dots" rather than "Duplicate *this* figure." This solution appears overexpansive if size is the only distortion, and if a breakdown in the gestalt is also reflected, it suggests poor judgment (see Fig. 7) —a cognitive lapse which raises the question of psychosis.

The maintenance of an even horizontal line is also of interest. The line may tend to drop downward in depression, slant up in denial, or see-saw up and down in a haphazard, uncontrolled way. The subject may stop to enlarge and elaborate, unable to sustain consistently even this simple repetitive activity. The reproduction of the double dot grouping appears pragmatically more significant when it *does* occur than when it does not, and suggests at the extreme a paranoid caution and suspiciousness, or more often obsessive-compulsive rigidity and concern for correctness and the tiny detail.

It should be added that the quality of the dot is expressive. As pointed out by the Gestalt psychologists, the loop is the first figure achieved developmentally, and in regression it is the form to which we return. The patient who loops on this figure is very apt to substitute loops for dots throughout (Fig. 38), or at the least on those figures which perturb him. Or in a variant pattern, the patient may adequately *copy* the dots, and then regress and loop on the recall.

There are other forms of the dot. There is the jabbed slashing dot

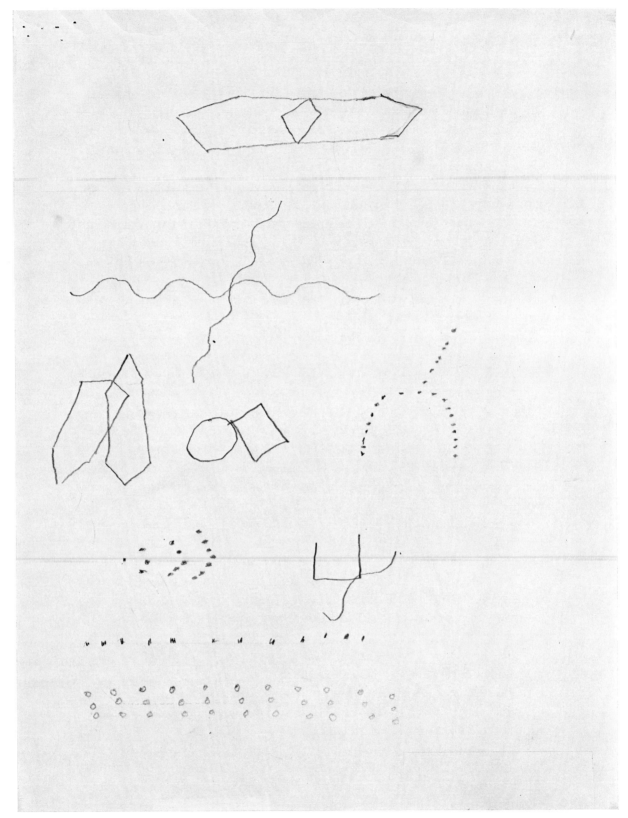

Figure 16.

or dash (Fig. 6) communicating very clearly the aggression it expresses. There is even what I consider a paranoid dot—a dot of such punctilious perfection and pointedness that it reflects a tension or need to be totally correct in order to ward off vague expectations of opprobrium. There is also the push-pull dot, which, like the hook on the end of letters in handwriting, suggests a particular polar patterning of aggression—of doing and undoing, lashing out and pulling back (Fig. 16). There is the looped dot with a contained inner figure, which suggests a capacity for fantasy elaboration that goes too far and indicates a potential for delusional or ideational symptom formation. (The equivalent for this can sometimes be caught on the WAIS Digit Symbol, where a certain kind of patient adds tiny dots to the interior of some of the patterns.) Finally, there is the variable, erratic downward squiggle, reflecting in Fred Brown's vivid phrase "the unravelling of defenses." All these variants may appear in the copy or recall of any of the figures demanding dots. And they may also appear wherever circles are called for.

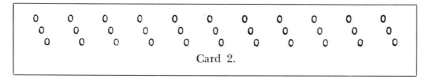

Card 2.

CARD 2

What I have said about the attributes of Card 1, in the context of size, quality of line, pressure, placement and order, which form the background consideration for every figure, leads to similar observations about Card 2. This has much in common with Card 1, but is more complex. It consists of eleven rows of evenly spaced columns of three circles slanting downward from left to right. The ability to maintain an even horizontal plane is more difficult in this figure, and the challenge to sustain measured distances with equal sized circles and equal angles can only be achieved by a balanced tension between vertical slant and horizontal ongoingness. Poor control is reflected in uneven size circles or in uneven line (Fig. 3). Depression may be suggested by a downhill slant, its denial by a rise, variability of mood or control by a wavering line.

During the copy phase, the attitude toward obvious deviations from the figure presented is also of interest: is it self-critical or self-accepting, perfectionist or a matter of indifference? The question of what the patient does with the circles—their evenness, shape, consistency—also requires a sustained control. On the recall, shifts occur to dots, slashes or loops. One patient, with real difficulty in accepting her femininity, converted these and other circles to squares (Fig. 17). Note also the difficulty that this same patient had with the circle on Card A and the phallicization of the breast figure on Card 4.

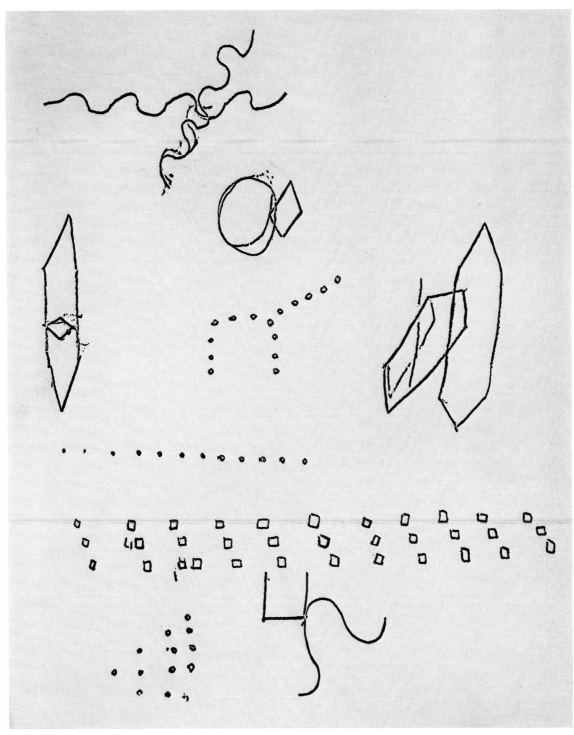

Figure 17.

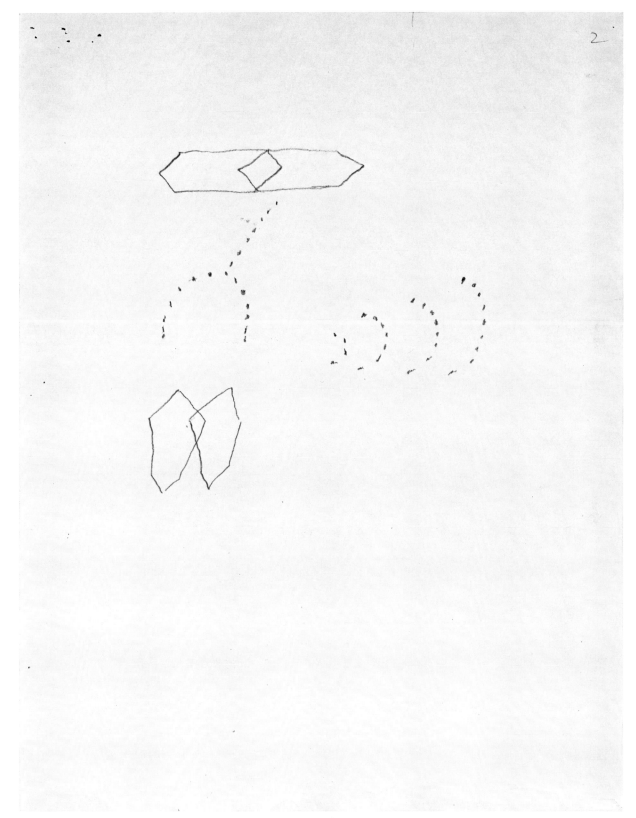

Figure 18.

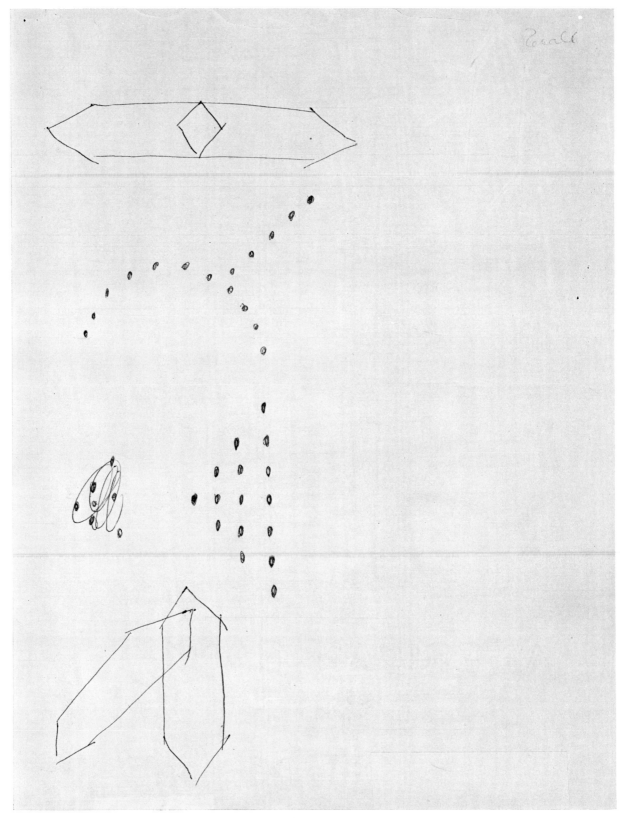

Figure 19.

The ongoingness of the design appears to stimulate patients who have difficulty in stopping. If perseverations occur, as they may in schizophrenics as well as organics, they are particularly apt to appear here and on Card 1.

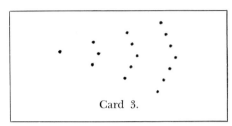

Card 3.

CARD 3

Card 3 is arrow-shaped, composed of dots fanning out on a horizontal axis. It appears to trigger unconscious aggressive impulses, and changes and distortions in the gestalt are frequent. One kind of patient, who has difficulty accepting and expressing his anger, may blunt the arrow until it is a diamond, or curve each line (Fig. 18) so that there is no threatening point. Another, who turns his aggression inward on himself, may reverse the direction or so outline the figure that the arrow *appears* reversed (Fig. 12) . A male transexual candidate, for whom an operation had been refused, presented a reversed figure a month before a successful autocastration (Fig. 19) . Others may sharpen the arrow to make it more pointed, suggesting an acceptance of their aggressivity, or express it covertly by arranging that the arrow collides with other figures.

A hint as to the ease with which aggression is tolerated, if not expressed, is often suggested in the recall where the arrow may be suppressed completely, be one of a very few recalled, or set far out of its natural place and order. Even minor changes are significant, one form seeming the equivalent of a stutter—a sharp break in the thrust forward and then a continuation of the figure, suggesting a need to pause and gather force before the expression of the impulse can be tolerated (Fig. 7) .

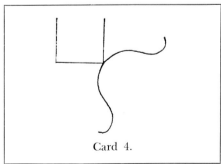

Card 4.

CARD 4

Card 4 presents an open-ended rectangle which exactly impinges on a curve. The curve appears to carry connotations of a breast, and

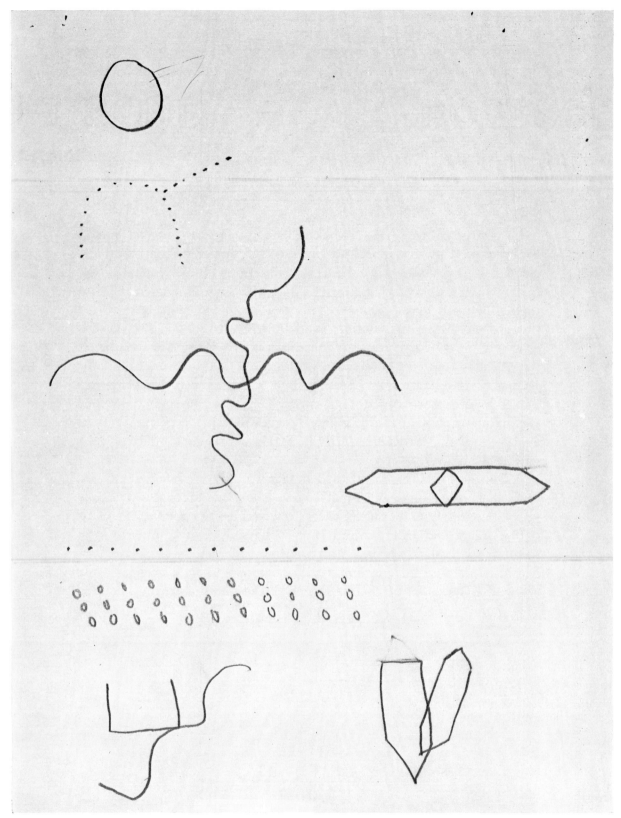

Figure 20.

Figure 21.

conjures up oral dependent material. The ease with which the curve
is drawn is important as an indication of the acceptance of one's oral
dependent needs, as is the neatness and facility of the joining of breast
and square. Schizoid people, who have difficulty in relating to others,
often leave a gap between square and breast. If this occurs on both
Card A and Card 4 (Fig. 11) sometimes distortions on Card 7 and the
the crossing of Card 6, a severe general contact problem seems probable. If the gap is most striking, or occurs only on Card 4, we infer that
it is the primary dependency relationship, the underlying oral need
which causes focal anxiety.

How and where the square and curve touch are also suggestive.
The peripheral touching, on the top curve or bottom, appears just
that: a peripheral relationship to the nurturing figure—a less flow-
ing breast, a less gratifying relationship. The inversion of the breast
shape has similar nongiving connotations (Fig. 20). Some subjects
penetrate the breast figure with the square. This has been called a
suicidal indicator (Fig. 21), on the ground that the oral needs are so
great as to constitute an assault on the nurturing environment: they
appear to spring from needs so insatiable, and pressed with such energy and such indifference to the boundary, that intolerable frustra-
tion is inevitable. Therefore, the depression, reinforced by the aggressive assaultive energy characterizing the intrusion, suggests a suicidal solution.

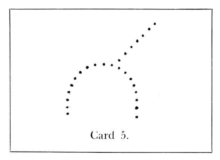

Card 5.

CARD 5

Card 5 may be copied or altered in a variety of ways. Even a moder-
ately compulsive or anxious person may feel compelled to count the
dots. As the severity of the anxiety mounts, so may the counting and
recounting, the doing and undoing. Lack of control, or anxiety about it,
or loss of equilibrium, may result in a tilting of the horseshoe (Fig.
22). Exorbitant dependency needs, often correlated with special treatment of the "breast" on Figure 4, may inflate the whole figure. Or oral
needs or fears of engulfment may widen the mouth of the figure so
that it attempts to take in greater territory (see Fig. 19).

Sexual preoccupation may result in penetrations into the curve, unconsciously equated with a vagina. On Figure 23 we see the Bender of
a menopausal (and badly disorganized) woman so preoccupied by

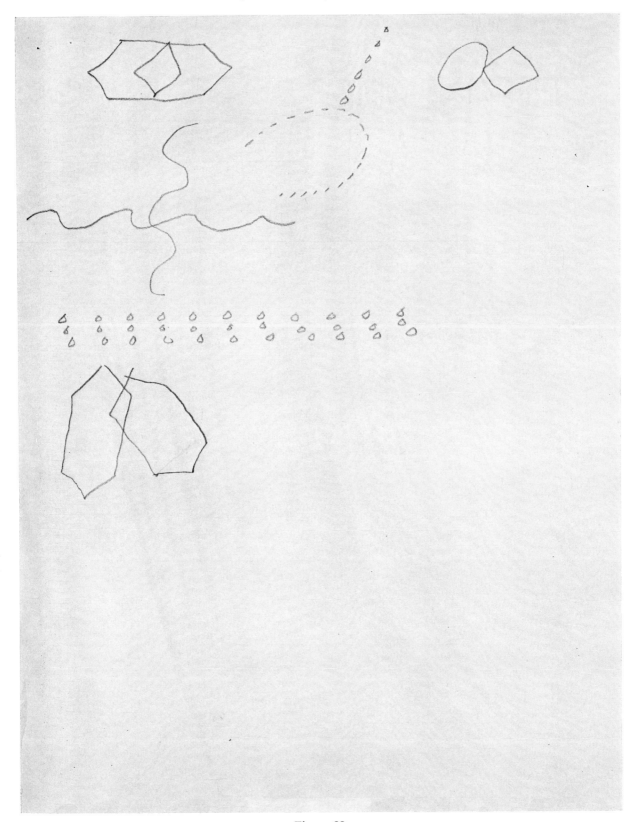

Figure 22.

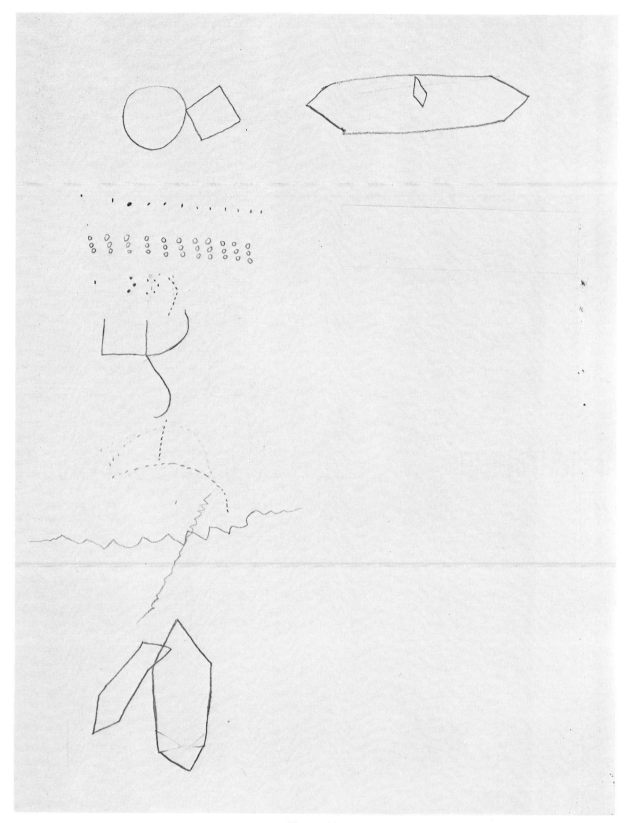

Figure 23.

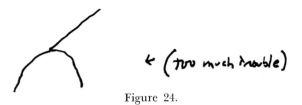

Figure 24.

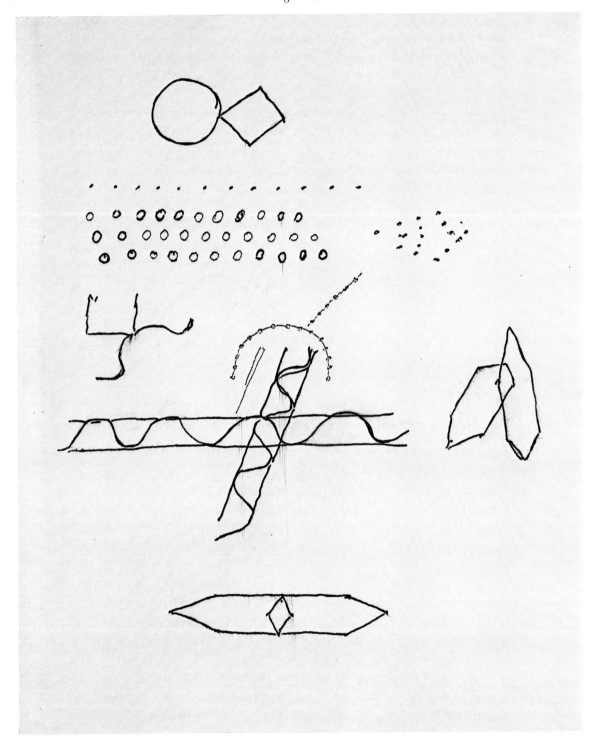

Figure 25.

sexuality and by what she experiences as loss of femininity, that almost every figure is affected. She cannot perform any of the curved figures but she does achieve this vaginal curve and then manages to place the phallic extension within it, instead of extending without.

Anxiety over masculinity or virility may be expressed by a drooping of the phallic extension. Or a denial of these anxieties or vaulting ambition in a male may be expressed by a reinforcement and special elevation. The same emphasis, in a woman, may reflect high ambition or competitive strivings. Gender difficulties of a more global order shift the feminine curve of the figure into an elongated phallic shape (Fig. 17).

Aggression, with special regard to sexuality, may be conveyed by a refusal to take time to make the dots, as in Figure 24. Or an obsessive-compulsive orientation may be conveyed by the familiar planning ahead—a sketched figure later reinforced by dots (Fig. 25).

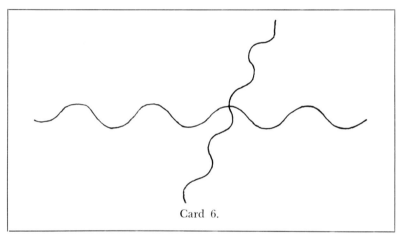

Card 6.

CARD 6

This card consists of two sinusoidal lines crossing at a slant. On one plane it may be conceived as a rudimentary figure drawing, with each area bearing the multilevelled symbolic freightage of the analogous area of the human figure. Thus the part of the vertical line above the horizontal reflects consciousness and control, that below the instinctual and unconscious. The extension to the left is fantasy-oriented, moving away from reality toward the past; to the right it is reality-oriented, an acting-out impulse directed at the environment.

Distortions along these continuums suggest the emphases above; or if the whole Bender series indicates that reaction formations and denial are dominant patterns, the distortions may suggest a recoil against the opposite pull. When most of the vertical line is below the horizontal, for example, a pull into the unconscious is usually indicated. But if the patient tends as a general rule to deny or repress, the exaggeration of the line above may express his resistance to the unconscious pull. As always, the significance of the particular depends on the general set.

The point at which the vertical line bisects the horizontal provides a clue as to the externalization or internalization of the subject's psychic drives. When the vertical moves left and the horizontal stretches out toward the right side of the page, a drive to act-out is indicated. When the vertical moves right, the reverse obtains. The drive is back into fantasy, a decathexis from the world, a withdrawal to inner life experience. This swing is well illustrated in the Serial Testing Chapter IV, by a comparison of this figure on the two Benders obtained from a manic depressive patient during the depressed and withdrawn state (Fig. 41b recall), with the figure produced in the manic, acting-out state (Fig. 42b recall).

Other facts such as ease or evenness of production, effortless on-goingness and spontaneity, reflect a strong self-confident ego, and a basic trust in one's ability to produce the acceptable, cope with the "ups and downs," confront what life may offer with minimal anxiety. In Figure 20 jerkiness of function and loss of ease is clear. There is a real difference between the flattening and lethargy of one who cannot give himself to the ongoing fluctuations of life mood (Fig. 26) and the painful inability to change direction characteristic of the organically impaired. (See Ch. 4.) This difficulty may take the form of a full stop at the top and bottom of each arc while the patient mobilizes consciously to change direction. Or the pencil may be lifted so that a series of dots at the change point are evident, while the patient "makes up his mind" as to what comes next. This is also noted during episodes of extreme confusion and anxiety, where literal reorientation seems necessary.

Other styles reflect other emphases and adaptations. The obsessive compulsive cannot afford spontaneity, and attempts to reproduce exactly—by many devices and rigid control—what is most suitably achieved by spontaneous flow. He plots, measures, graphs, does and undoes (Fig. 25). Some patients require structure and underpinning for most figures, others confine it to those most anxiety-producing. Where aggression is prominent a hostile slashing denial of commitment to the task distorts and flattens, so that only the rough gestalt remains (Fig. 6) or the aggression may be masked so that a careless line cross results.

The decrease in the height and depth of the curves suggests flattened affect or a fear of yielding to the emotional experience of permitting oneself to respond to mood changes. Anxiety may be expressed in a shaky hesitant line or reinforcement (Fig. 27). Special difficulty with one part of the pattern is significant. The patient who cannot leave the top of the transverse line alone is anxious and preoccupied about

Figure 26.

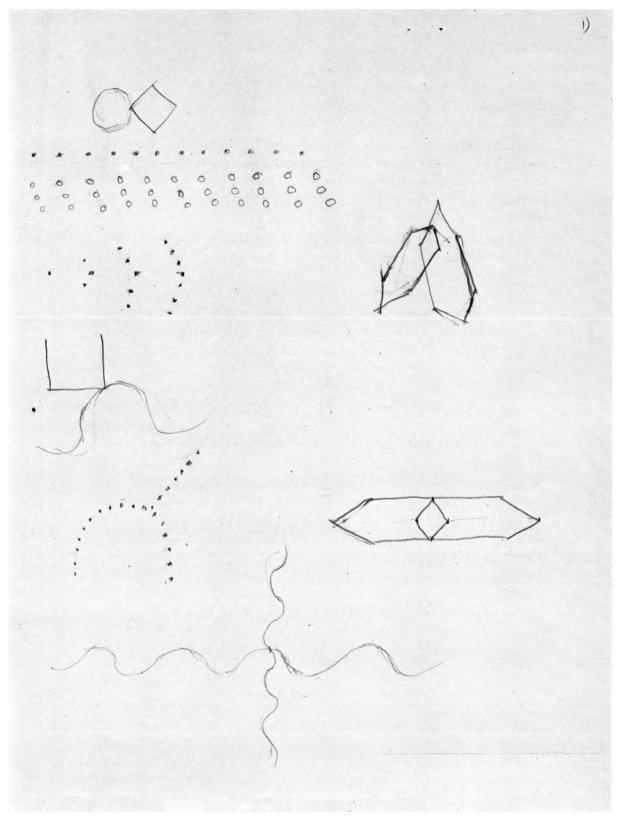

Figure 27.

control and coping, and intellectual function (Fig. 25) . Compare him with the patient who emphasized the lower half, who is perhaps too open to the pull of the unconscious, whose repressive barriers are weakening, or who is experiencing instinctual problems.

An interesting question is the point at which the line crosses. In this figure, as in others, it has implications for the ease or difficulty of contact in interpersonal relations. Some patients must *plot* the crosspoint, making a tiny mark and then constructing radial lines above and below, which suggests a lack of spontaneity and a need for constant monitoring and forethought—planned interaction. Others cannot even perceive the lines as crossing, and construct two curvy V's, thus eliminating the need to cross, truly to take on and effect a relationship. They prefer the tangential, the more tentative contact and retreat, or in extreme cases they fear any contact at all, and are unable to effect it.

Except in extraordinary cases, and even then rarely, this is usually seen only in the recall. It may take the form of blotting out of one line and reproducing only the other (Fig. 28) . When a patient can recall only the horizontal line, the omission of the vertical suggests not only the contact problem of the crossover but difficulty in accepting and integrating the conscious and unconscious with ongoing experience. This may arise either from failing repression, and a consequent need to blot out the unconscious completely, or from sharpening conflicts between conscious and unconscious goals. Occasionally this results in a curious braiding of the lines, an inability to distinguish one sphere from another so that only the horizontal axis is retained (Fig. 29) .

The quality of line is also revealing. Anxious patients, afraid to commit themselves lest they be wrong, *sketch* the line, so that many interpretations become possible (see Fig. 27) . And as noted, the aggression and impetuosity of others is evident in the dark slashing figures, which show minimum regard for reproducing the figure presented.

There are, in addition, idiosyncratic representations—a sharp downturning or lopping off of the horizontal line, which appears as an interruption in the ongoingness of life, and in the acceptance of the future and the responsibility of coming to terms with the environment. Supported by evidence from other quarters the sharpness of the shift may presage a depression or a suicidal attempt. Scissoring of the lines, with the lower line rising toward the horizontal, suggests the upsurge of the unconscious, repressive failures, and the contamination of consciousness by what lies below. A more nearly right-angled figure may reflect the need to compartmentalize, the wish for optimal distance between what is above and what below.

And there are always the contaminations, fascinating in their end-

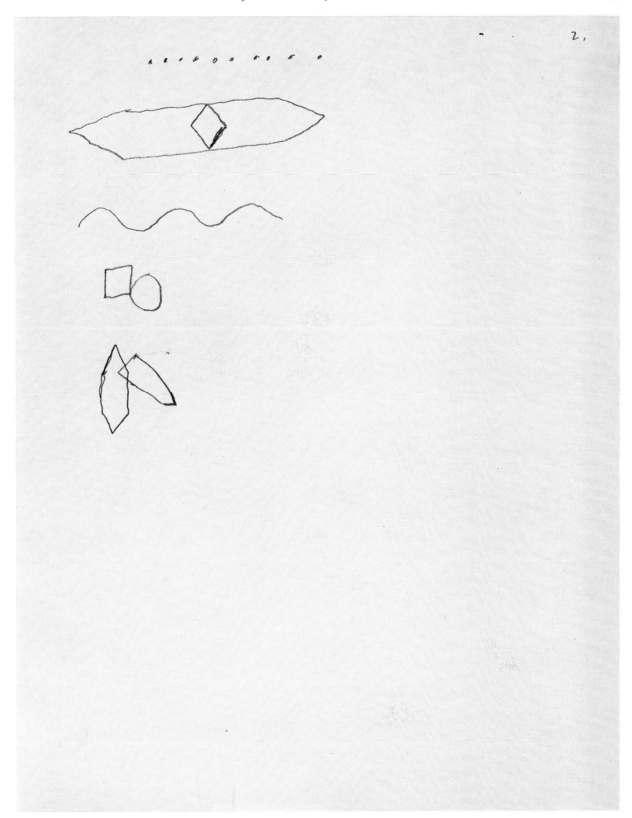

Figure 28.

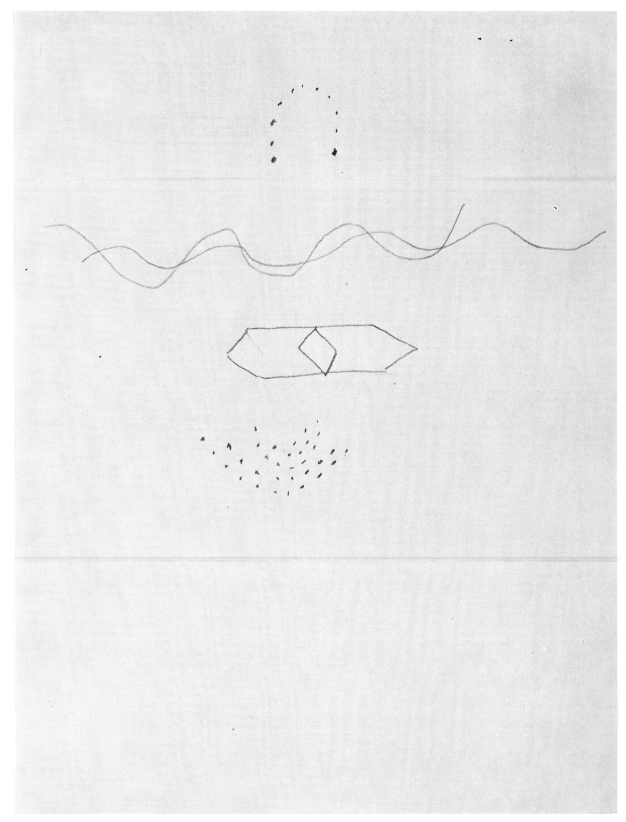

Figure 29.

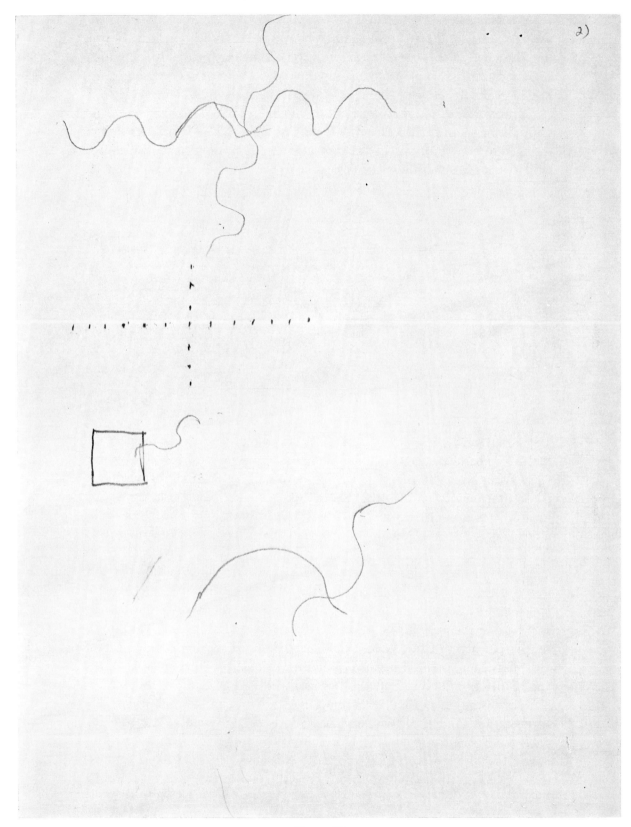

Figure 30.

less variety, where a patient fuses two figures. For example, Figure 30, where Card 1 and Card 6 have been combined. Here the difficulties of the card are denied by straightening the curves (probable difficulty with femininity) and by avoiding the flow (fear of spontaneity and loss of control). This patient was so disorganized that her recall contained several contaminations, most of them related to curves. Contaminations confined to the distortions of one particular figure has a more limited significance than multiple contaminations seen here, which suggest diffuse confusion on a psychotic level, with a pervasive boundary loss, perseverations, and inability to maintain intact the integrity of any figure.

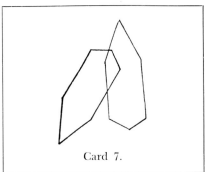

Card 7.

CARD 7

Card 7, with its leaning, mutually interlaced trapezoidal shapes, is a stimulating figure. Like Card A, it summons up associations to interpersonal interactions, primary dependency relationships or elaborations from that to other later interactions. The original dependency configuration determines the quality of all later relationships. It establishes the capacity for basic trust, in others and one's self—the ability to expect and accept appropriate help from others, and to offer, without pain and a sense of deprivation, appropriate support.

Variations in the affective quality of basic dependency configuration may be expressed by qualitative changes in the copy which express the color of the relationship, hint at the gender identity of the figures involved. Here we find the minor lengthenings, shortenings, widenings, or sharpenings, in this objectively most difficult of the Bender cards. But more fundamental distortions reflect significant shifts in the meaning of the interaction, and the possibilities appear endless.

This figure, like Figure 6, lends itself to an anthropomorphic interpretation, and the same interpretations as those noted in the discussion of Figure 4 apply. Here, however, we are limited to the vertical analogies—specifically, the associations of interacting figures. The objective difficulty of reproducing this complex figure appears to promote distortions even on the copy. The ability to reproduce without change the pointed top and bottom of each figure, and the respective size and angle of impingement of the two figures, suggest relatively conflict-resolved parent-child relationship and, by inference, progress toward, or achievement of, relative autonomy.

But usually distortions do occur, and the treatment of the points—either at the top, in the cognitive control area, or at the bottom, in the instinctual sphere—is suggestive. Inability to close the points may suggest an openness to influence, or seepage—a loss of control over the instinctual—or the crossing of the point lines may suggest strenuous efforts to maintain control. Elongated points, especially when executed in dark slashing lines, may express overt hostility or a potential for violence. In addition it indicates that the patient has problems in coping with masculinity.

The point at which the figures impinge may also be illuminating. The supporting figure may become almost a missile intruding from without (Fig. 31), sometimes from above—as the conflict presents as an obsessive preoccupation; sometimes in the middle—as a body blow. Or the connection may be shifted to the bottom of the figure, suggesting an inappropriate, regressive, primitive instinctual involvement (Fig. 32). The distance between the bottom points may be widened, so that the left, dependent figure swings up almost at right angles. Assuming the figures to represent a parent-child relationship, this suggests a reinforcement of the need to keep separate that which should not be together. Or, one may see it as a reaction formation against a prohibited attraction, in Fred Brown's phrase, the 'incestuous configuration.' Figure 26 is an illustration from a girl whose incestuous experience is documented.

The kinds and degree of dependency may be expressed in the angle at which the figures overlay each other and as well in the relative size of the figure. The patient may experience himself as small, weak, totally dependent on a large, even threatening figure. Or he may see himself as an insupportable burden, asking more than the parent has to offer, in fact, as the guilty instrument of parental collapse (Fig. 33). He may see himself as almost engulfed by an essentially hostile, rejecting figure, or he may feel himself intolerably weighed down by the demands of exactly the person to whom he legitimately looks for support (Fig. 12).

At times, the demands of the supporting figure may be internalized, surviving as an obsessive idea or introject (see Fig. 31). The affective flavor of the relationship may be indicated in the increase or decrease of the overlap, in the context of the slant, or in the sharpness or tentativeness of line, the heaviness or lightness of the contact points, the ease or exaggerated angularity of the corners. A relationship characterized by hostility may be expressed by jabbing, intrusive protrusions into the parent body—or by the parental body into the "other" (Fig. 34).

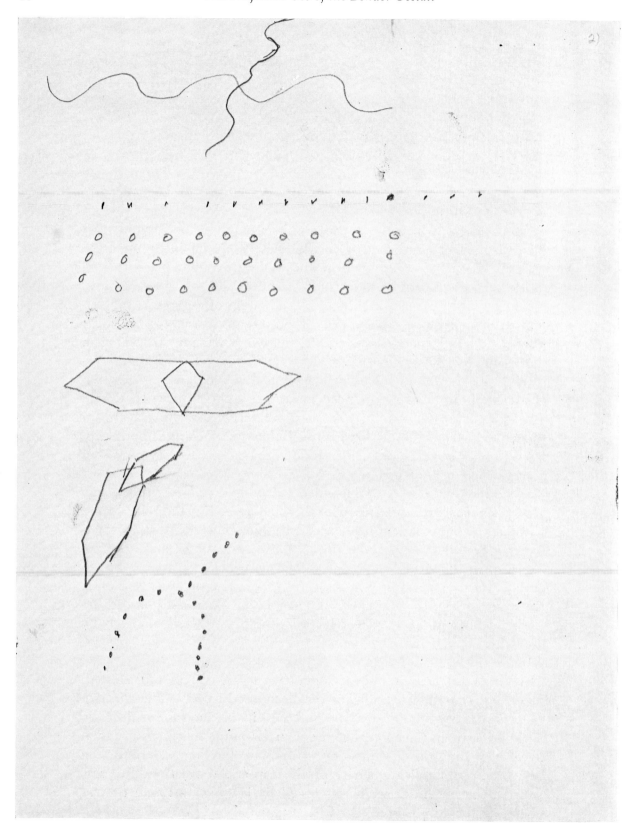

Figure 31.

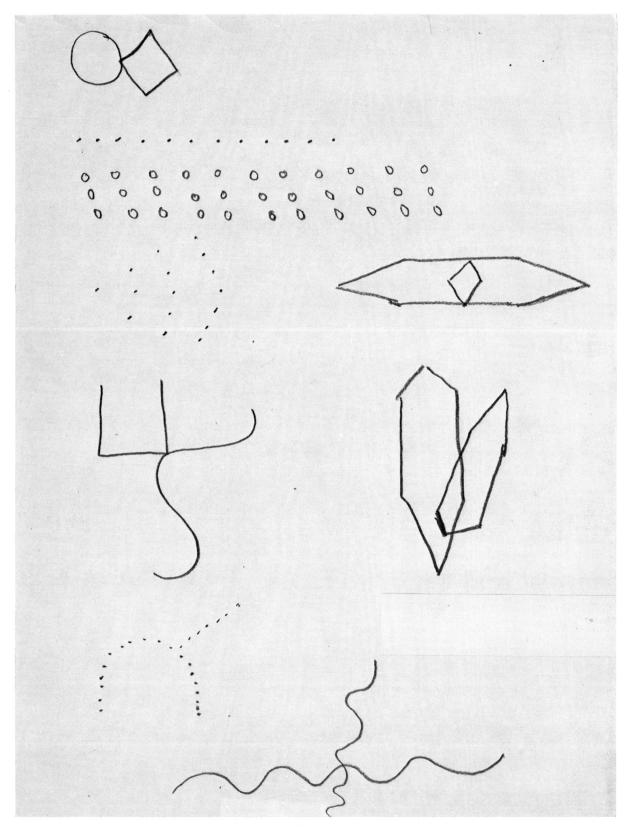

Figure 32.

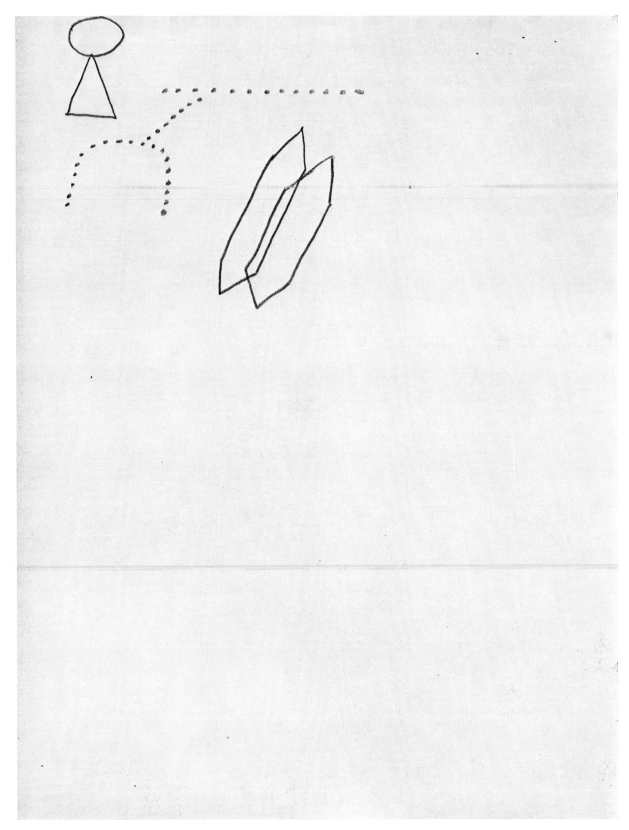

Figure 33.

Figure 34.

Thus the patient may indicate a variety of experiences: that he is being engulfed by the 'supporting' figure; is fixed in a symbiotic relationship; penetrated and hurt by the sharp projections from the parent figure; or barely supported at all. Both trapezoids may be drastically altered, suggesting that the relationship is a destructive, disturbing one. Thus, in Figure 35, all angled ends are omitted, suggesting a critical, mutually destructive interaction which both castrates and renders those involved unable to control; and in Figure 36 the dependent figure must sacrifice its integrity of form in order to achieve a relationship at all.

In the comparison of copy and recall, hidden aspects of the relationship, which are often controlled by overtly well-functioning patients, may be dramatically uncovered. Note for example, the sequence of Figures 37 and 38. The first with the excellent, if (as we infer from other figures) slightly anxious, slightly regressed copy represents the healthy facade. And the recall first presents an adequate dependent pair. But the patient cannot maintain this set. The defenses collapse, and he adds a curious distortion, or confabulation, with Bender Figure A, in which paired, overlapping figures, one cut in half, the other a completely truncated and "castrated" figure, suggest the complex, hostile and fearful, guilt-laden relationship under the effective defensive facade.

Dependency relationships appear to provide the substrate of the experience evoked by this figure, but they may, of course, be overlaid by other relationships which echo the first or are reactions against

Figure 35.

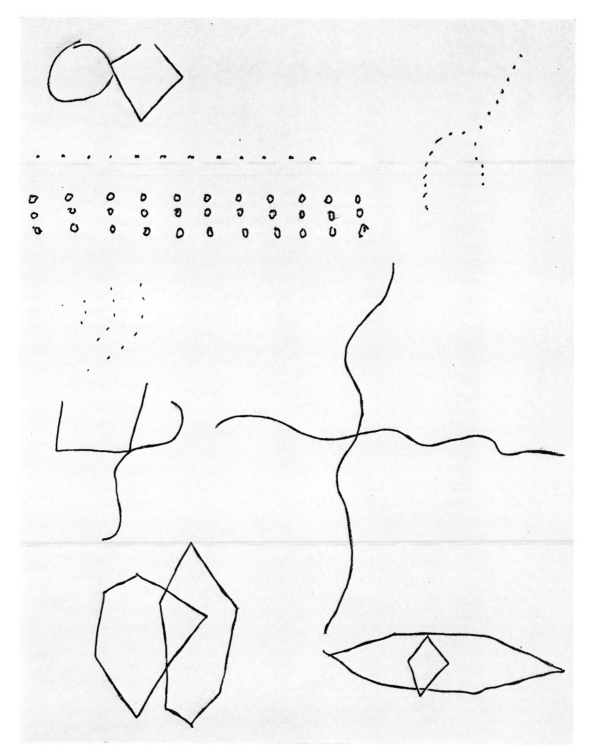

Figure 36.

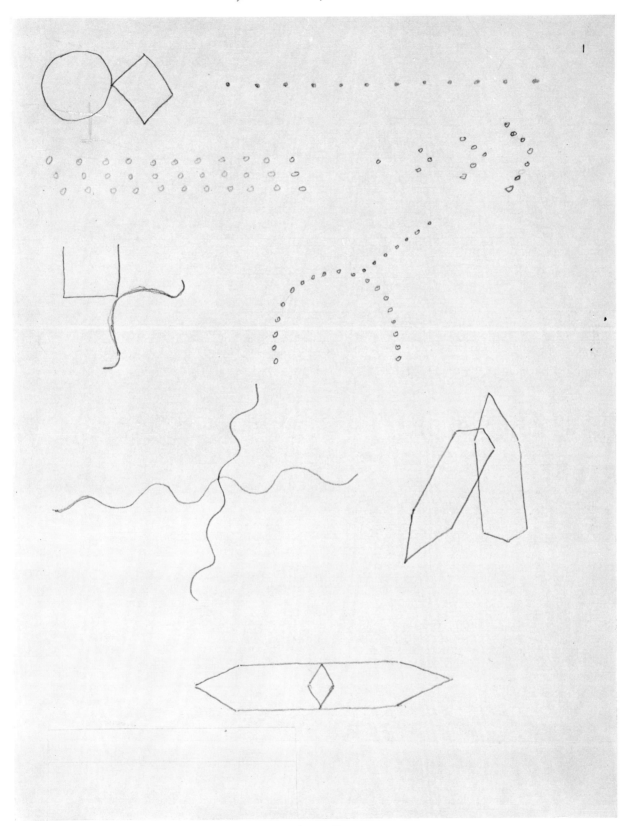

Figure 37.

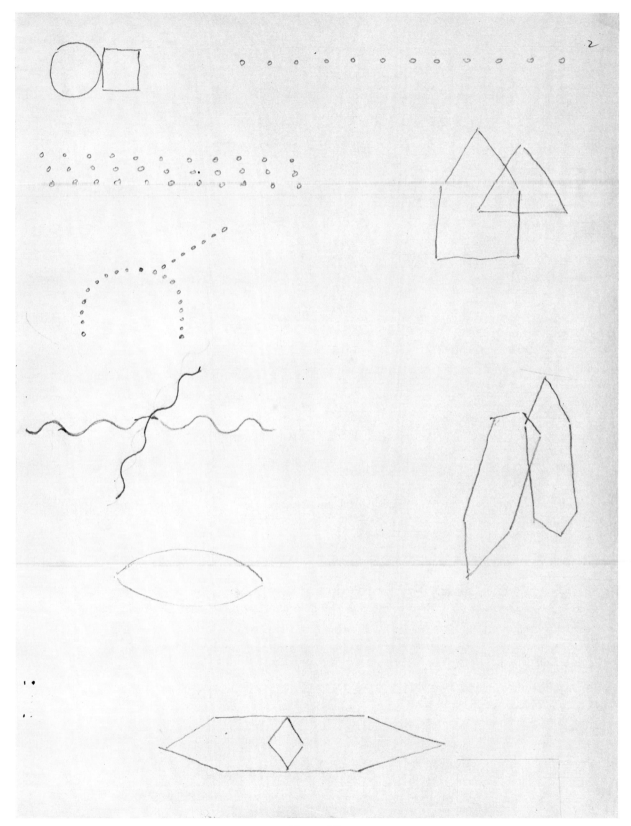

Figure 38.

it. Twinning or side-by-side positioning may express a homosexual trend—a fear of the "other," a like to like preference (Fig. 18).

We omit here a discussion of those patients who, by reason of organic rather than functional limitation, find it difficult to achieve a connection between any two figures, and whose performance throughout reflects to a greater or lesser degree these special juxtaposition problems. Instances of this may be found in Chapter V on the organically impaired, for example Figure 45.

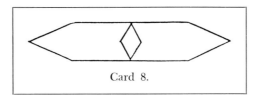

Card 8.

CARD 8

The final Figure 8 in the series is of a trapezoid enclosing a centered diamond. Its place as the last card in the series is a little like Card X, the "summary" card of the Rorschach. It may recapitulate problems suggested by earlier figures. But it also sometimes summons up a residual determination to improve or to perform adequately, and it is in any event not so difficult as some of the other figures and is therefore less subject to distortion and somewhat less rich in projective cues.

The figure may be elongated, giving it a phallic emphasis, or made short and fat—a feminization (Fig. 22). The angularity of the figure offers opportunities to convey attitudes toward masculinity: to close neatly, to leave stabbing protrusions (Fig. 6), be unable to close (Fig. 19), to patch (Fig. 31), to shrink in size relative to other figures (Fig. 50b), or to find it necessary to reinforce the closing in various ways (Fig. 10). From the choice made, we deduce an ease in accepting masculinity; a lack of ease which is overcompensated, even to the extent of confusing masculinity and violence (Fig. 6); a draining of the instinctual with fears of loss of vitality and even of impotence; or an urgency in relation to instinctual pressures which requires special binding and control.

Another aspect of the figure is the size and placement of the small diamond within the larger frame. Is it tiny, inconsequential in relation to the field, or swollen so that it dominates its environment? Is it centered, as in the original, or moved toward the right or left? The leftward movement suggests a withdrawal, a movement toward fantasy, away from reality, and in some cases regression. And the rightward tendency suggests a wish to move out into the environment, or a push toward awareness.

The ease with which the diamond fits into the larger figure ap-

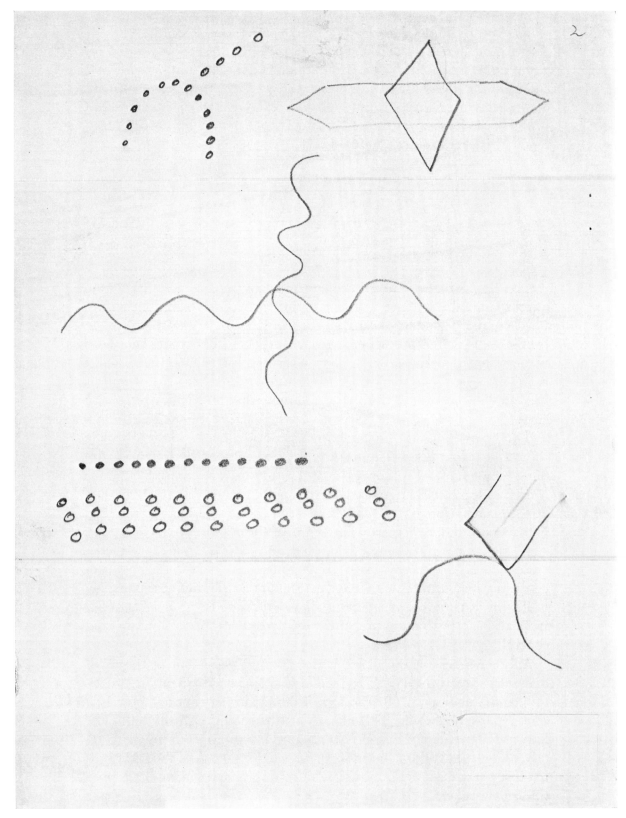

Figure 39.

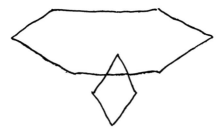

Figure 40.

pears related to the self-percept in relation to the environment and offers clues as to reality testing, and boundary problems, or perhaps to the "observing ego" in relation to the psyche. One patient in recall plastered a diamond on top of the main figure (Fig. 39), completely ignoring the demands of the situation, the boundary definition. He ignored the ground in an egocentric concentration on the figure. Others permit the diamond to float, out of anchoring contact, as if confused as to the reality requirements and lost and helpless in relation to them. Or the diamond appears to be falling out of the trapezoid, dropping out of contact in the most literal way (Fig. 40).

Chapter 3

SERIAL TESTING

HAVING considered the projective significance of the Bender figures individually and as a group, let us look now to the usefulness of the test in reflecting change over time. This function is frequently pertinent in assessing therapeutic progress. As an example, we will compare the Benders of a manic depressive patient seen in two separate hospitalizations, three years apart.

The original Bender (Fig. 41a) was, to begin with, the most microscopic I have seen. In its well preserved form, consistent miniature scale, it reflected both the patient's intelligence and her control—her rigid, exacting standards, paranoid apprehension, and obsessive-compulsive life style. The scale, the order, the organization express at once her consuming need to control, and also the rage that lies beneath it. And, above all, it communicates her depression. The rage is turned back on herself (note the way the supporting guidelines of the arrow figure completely reverse the direction of impact). The self-hate, guilt and abysmal self-esteem are expressed in the shrunken life space, the inability to give or to take legitimate space, the pinchy, self-denying watchfulness required by this kind of performance. The recall at this time is on the same scale (Fig. 41b).

Three years later, the patient appears in a manic phase. She starts off loosely and carelessly; she has shed the need to inhibit, to program, to order, to hold back. Figure a is planted squarely and spontaneously in midspace, with no thought to the overall problem of fitting the figures to the space allotted. Then she proceeds impressionistically, neither checking the number of the dots on Figure 1 nor (when it bores her) bothering to complete them (Fig. 42a1). After drawing Bender Figure 3, she jumps illogically to the top of the page and draws Figures 5 and 6, still hastily simplifying, and disregarding reality demands as represented by the page, in favor of following her compelling inner impulse. Then she lets go completely and expands so that Figures 7, 8, and 9 each take a whole page (Figs. 42a 2, 3, 4). The contrast between this explosive, self-indulgent, erratic and grandiose performance and the early microscopic set is dramatic, and vividly demonstrates the manic depressive alternation of mood.

On the recall of the retest, the patient cannot be bothered to dredge up more than three figures, and each is projectively revealing. The first, the aggressive arrow, is rotated upward as if exploding. The second, the crossed lines, is expansive and outer-directed, demonstrating the release of energy. Compare the crossover points of Figure 6 on

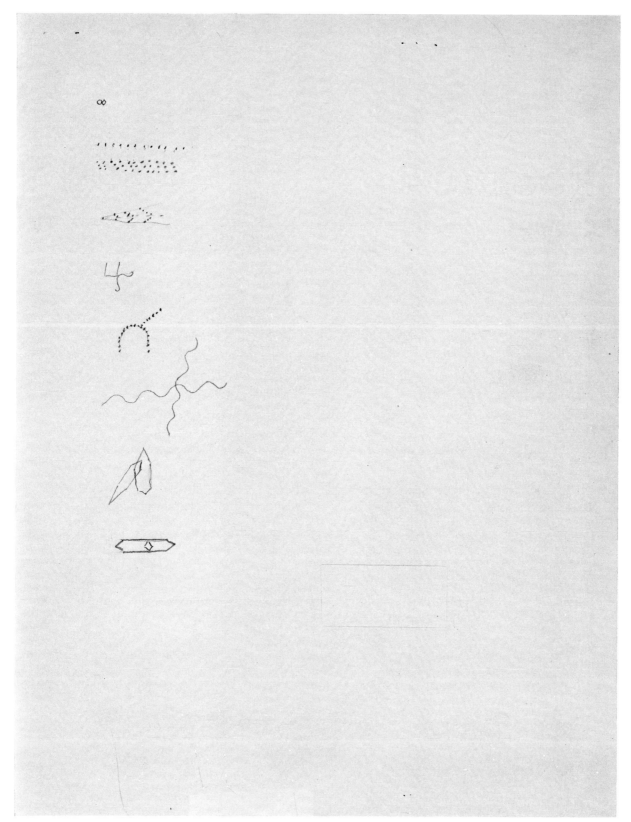

Figure 41a.

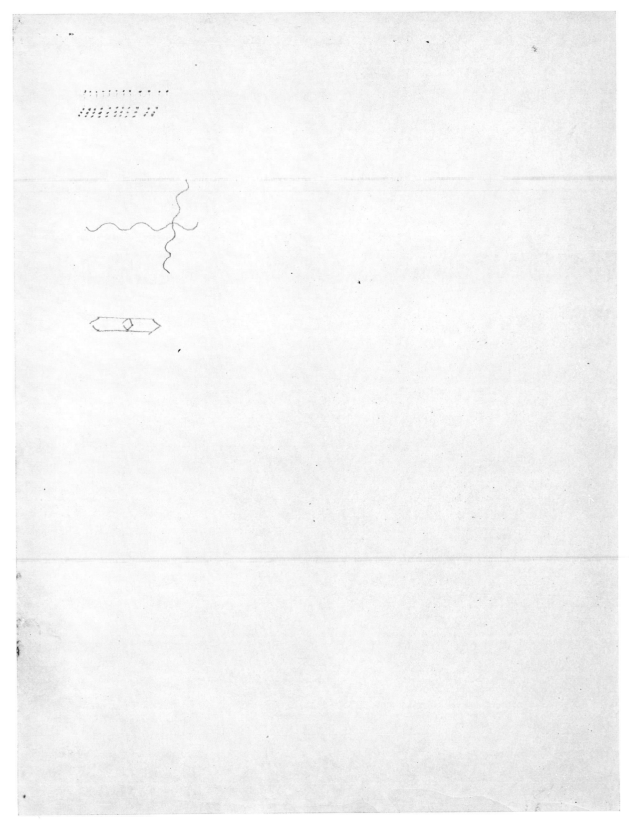

Figure 41b.

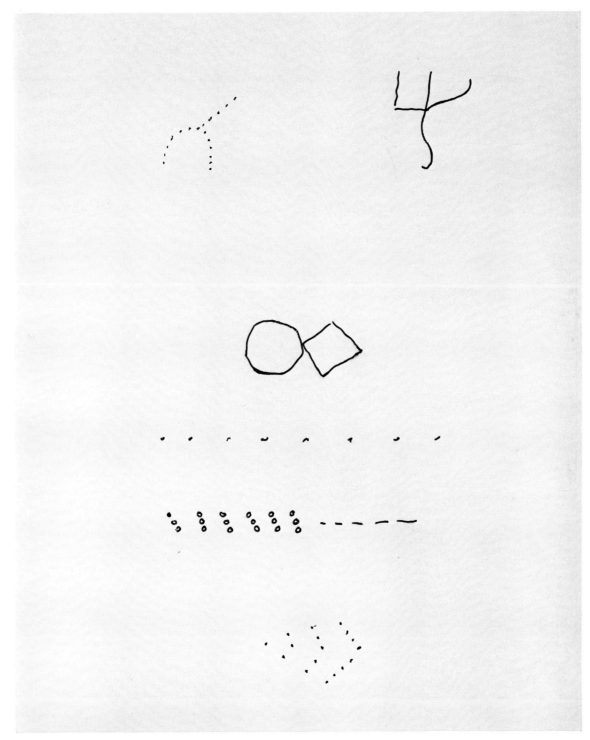

Figure 42a1.

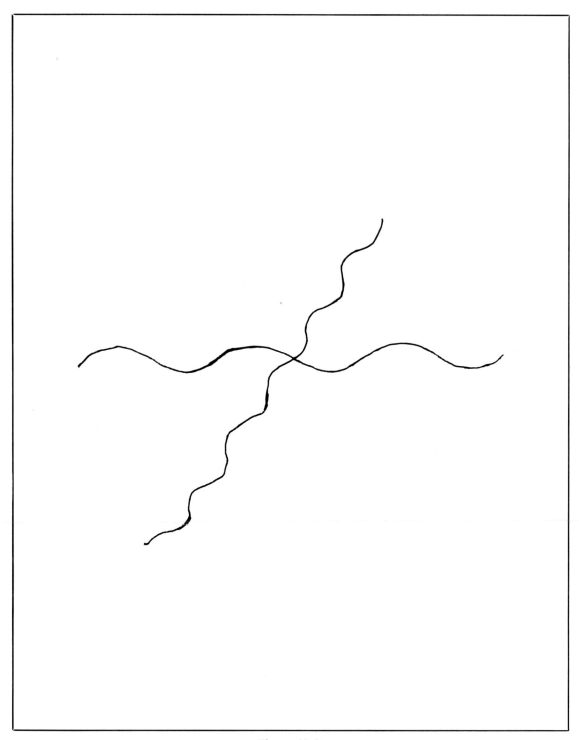

Figure 42a2.

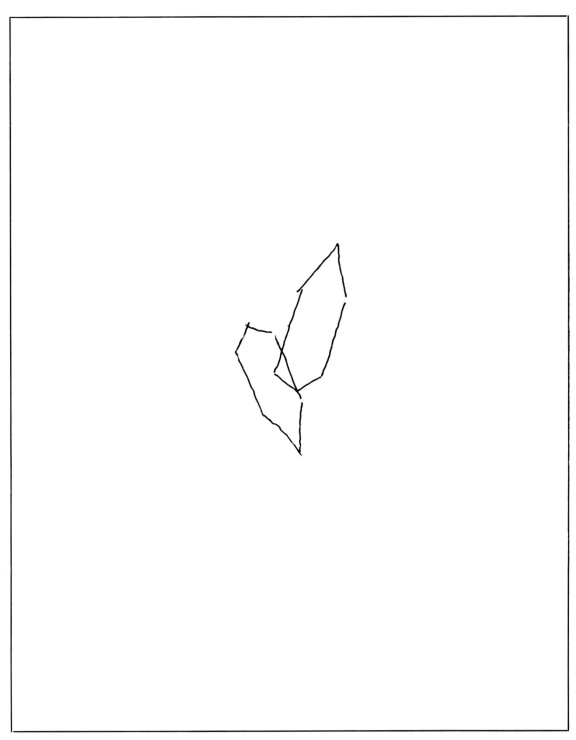

Figure 42a3.

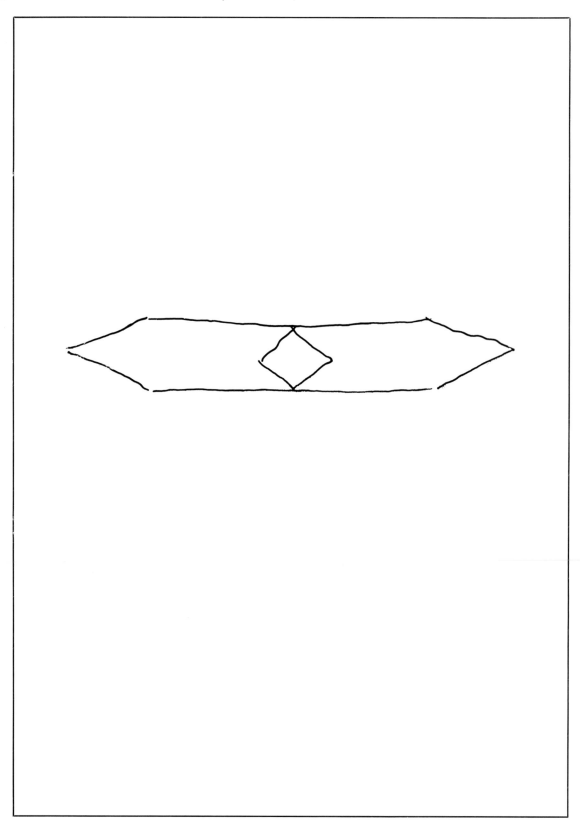

Figure 42a4.

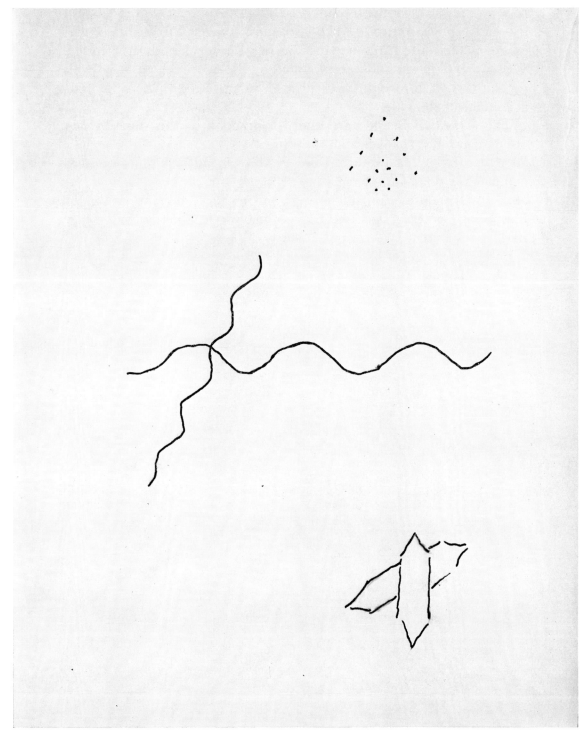

Figure 42b.

the recall of the first depressed set (Fig. 41b) with the manic recall set. On the first set (Fig. 41b), the crossover point is at the right, the "pull" back and inward. On the second (Fig. 42b) the point is to the left and the pull explodes outward. The last figure recalled, Bender Figure 7, expresses the underlying despair: the two leaning figures are crossed, the self-figure is wiped out, obliterated by the figure which usually offers support. A distortion this depressed, in an acting-out setting, hints at a suicidal potential.

The sequential Benders are rarely as dramatic as this. But they do often reflect the changes and continuities of the therapeutic course. Each one bears the characteristic "hand" of the performer, just as handwriting does. But changes are reflected, not simply developmentally or in response to organic change, but in affect and the waxing or waning of ego strengths. The changes may occur spontaneously over time, in response to stress or in the course of therapy.

Chapter 4

ORGANICALLY IMPAIRED AND
CONFUSIONAL BENDERS

A NUMBER of Benders are presented here which are outside the mainstream of this discussion. They include the Benders of two organically impaired patients, and two of the confusional state of a long-term drug user. They are intended to provide contrast and to suggest limits beyond which the projective emphasis is not of central significance.

Figures 43a & b, 44, 45, 46, and 47 are the Benders of brain damaged patients which were chosen because they are unequivocal and illustrate a number of the characteristic distortions of this group. Obviously, not all the brain damaged—particularly the minimally impaired—are as obligingly classic as this. But these examples will serve to alert the clinician to less obvious cases where the Bender shows a tendency, or single deviation of one of the organic patterns we see here.

In brief, where organicity is suspected, we look for a number of things: the tendency to rotate a figure counterclockwise; the overall regressive trend (seen often in the shift from dots to loops and in the primitivization of figures; the difficulty in changing direction; the tendency to complete—that is, close the open figure; the perseverations; the problem of achieving juxtaposition, with parts of a figure or interlocking figures either casually separated, or forced together by peculiar figure-distorting protrusions. And we see the loss of gestalt, on the recall especially, but also on the copies.

Figures 48a & b, and 49a & b (copy and recall) are the productions of two long-term drug users in a confusional state. These Benders are often difficult, if not impossible, to distinguish from schizophrenic Benders, without supporting evidence, forewarning or hindsight. But they are perhaps drawn more deliberately in accordance with some inner but consistent principle not related to the Bender itself. Certainly, they go far beyond the instruction to "copy the figures," to an elaboration and interweaving of them. But they reflect both an indifference to reality demands and an inner vision perhaps—or at least intricacy of organization rather than its lack. And a certain level of consistency and purposiveness does prevail.

Nevertheless, most of us, not forewarned, might be tempted to see them as one vast schizophrenic concoction in which grandiosity and ideas of relationship play a prominent part. A comparison of these figures with that of the paranoid schizophrenic in Figure 4 demonstrates the

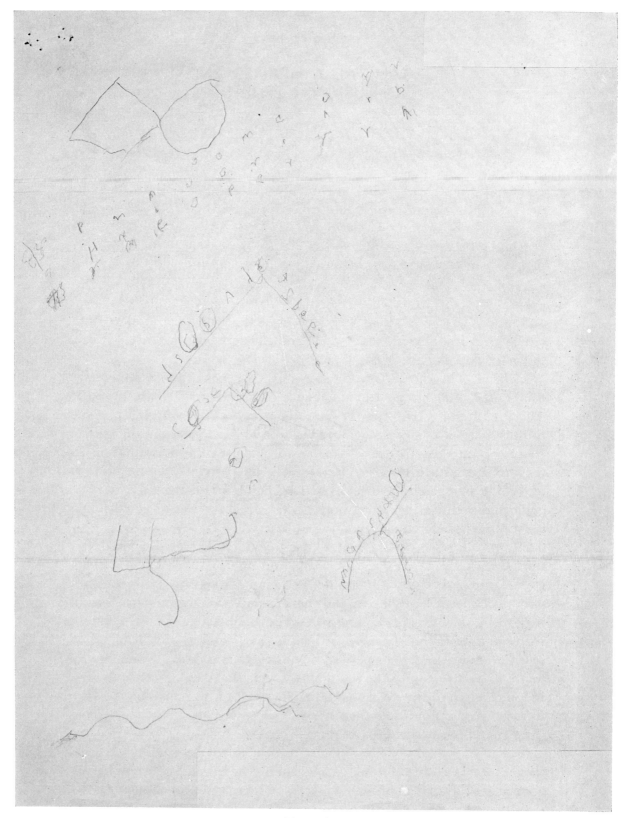

Figure 43a.

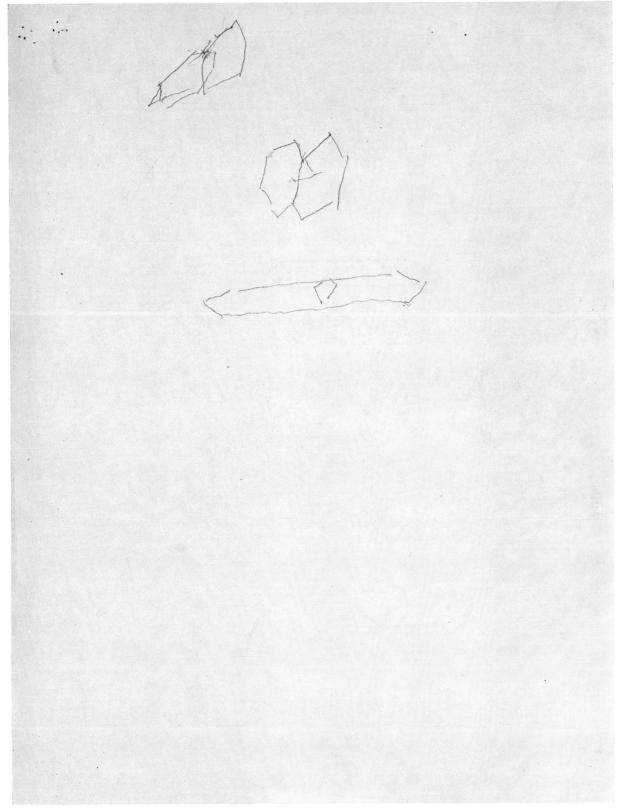

Figure 43b.

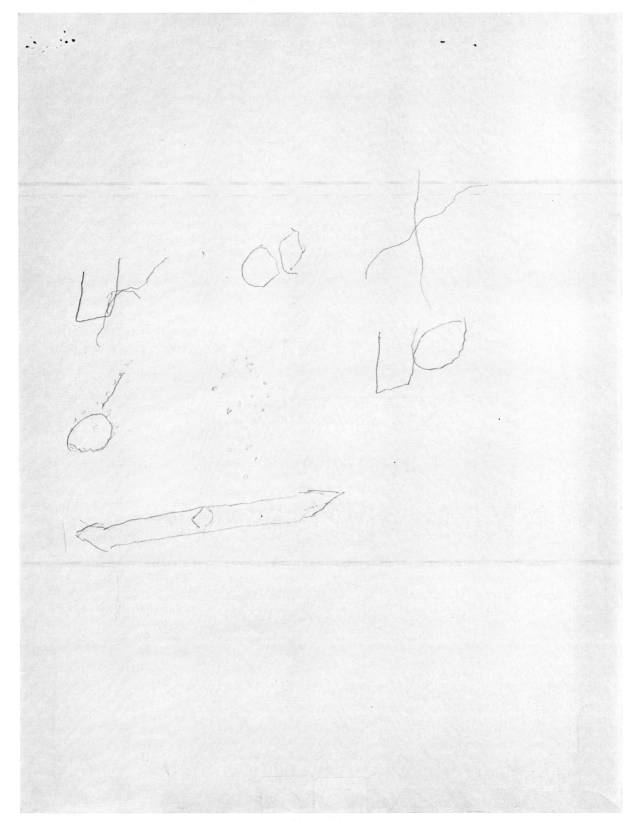

Figure 44.

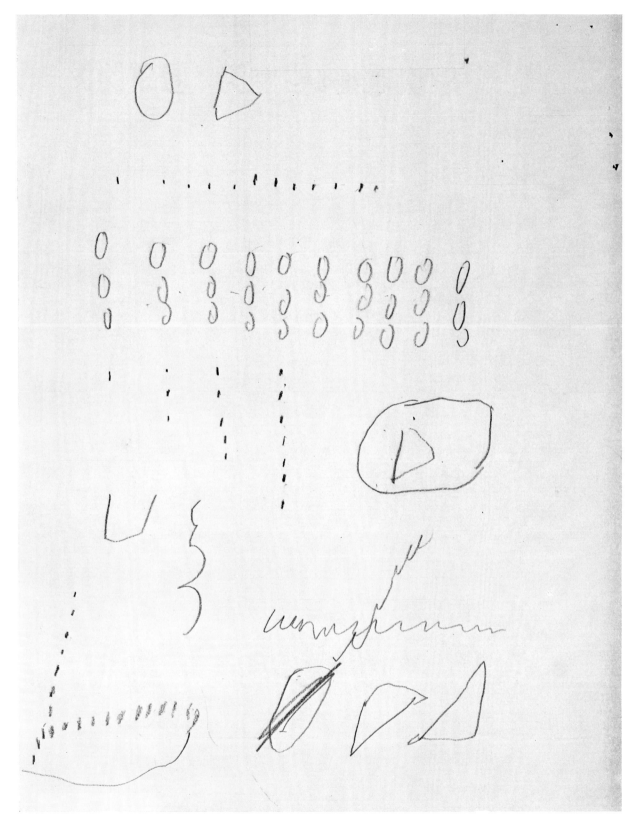

Figure 45.

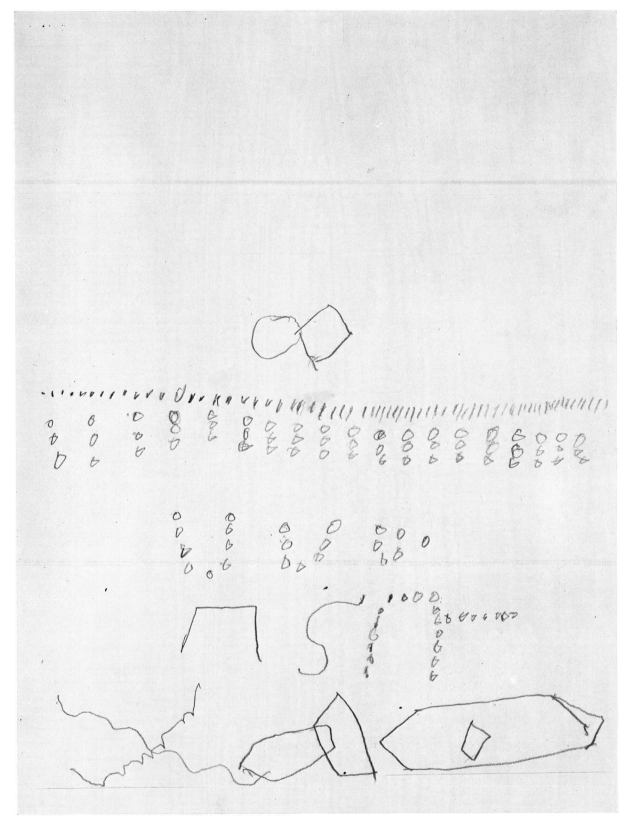

Figure 46.

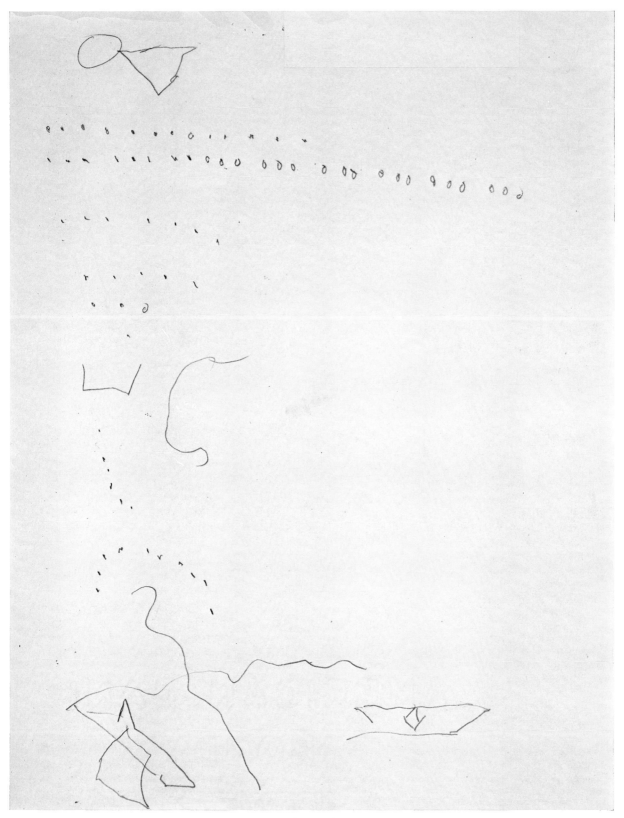

Figure 47.

Figure 48a.

Figure 48b.

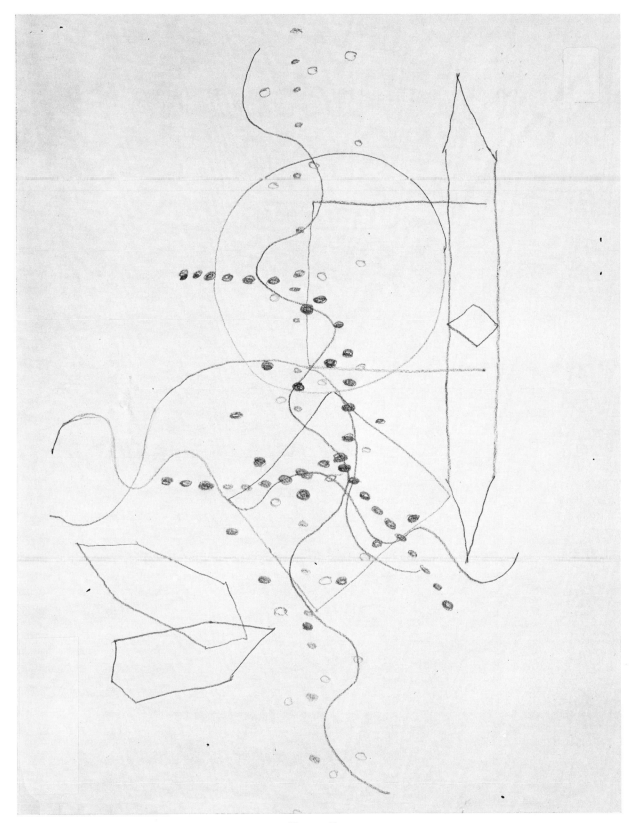

Figure 49a.

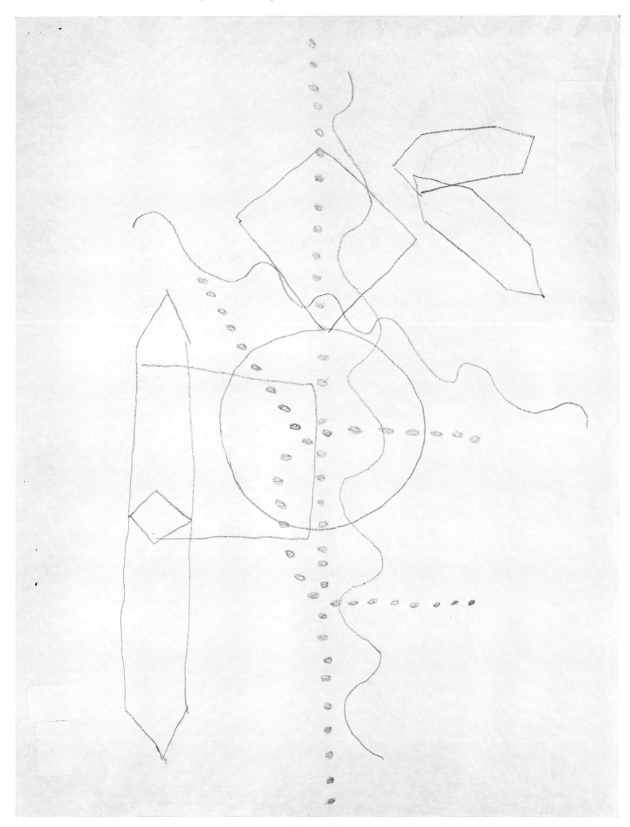

Figure 49b.

difficulty of differential diagnosis, and the need to rule out, or at least be aware of, the possibility of a drug effect before drawing diagnostic conclusions.

Chapter 5

THE OVERALL VIEW: STYLE, THEMATIC EMPHASIS AND CONTAMINATIONS

TO sum up: The foregoing pages present the author's view of what the "pull" of each Bender card is. And the illustrative material demonstrates some of the ways in which these thematic evocations produce distortions in both copy and recall which shed light on the subject's inner life. There is no intent to give these notes a hard and fast validity. Rather it is hoped to communicate an attitude which will encourage the examiner to add this test to his projective battery.

Besides the symbolic significance of the individual figures one is struck by the overall consistency of each person's performance, and this summary chapter will discuss some of the consistencies which illustrate that aspect.

Frequently, for example, light is shed on the subject's life style, or more specifically on his coping and defensive mechanisms. The hysteric may drop in the recall the figures which disturb him. The obsessive compulsive will attempt to organize, in a rational, appropriate, adaptive way, by a simple logical sequence; or, in decompensation, in a way that demonstrates the erosion of the defense (see Fig. 51). He may organize compulsively, at the expense of the integrity of any particular figure, putting each figure, regardless of its spatial requirements, into a box (Fig. 7). Or he may start with the intention of separating figures and hold to what originally served to separate, such as a line or other division, while losing sight of the goal (Fig. 4). Or a particular defensive maneuver such as doing and undoing may be reflected in the subject's absolute need to strike out and redo—often change without improvement—(Fig. 50).

An oral dependent quality and regressive pull may pervade the series, with minor deviations on the copy becoming exaggerated on the recall. In this kind of series the heterosexual, centered contact of Bender Figure A may shift toward the top, to the oral sphere, with an open sucking contact point. In the related Bender Figure 4 the breast may be slightly or deeply penetrated by the oral demanding contact of the square. Dots may be changed to regressive loops. The difficult interaction on Bender Figure 7 may be changed into a hanging, overtly dependent relationship on the "self" side. Or it may be expressed more subtly, as a sense of being weighed down by the normally supporting figure. This kind of person easily registers as excessive demands from without.

An aggressive drive may be expressed throughout (see Figs. 3, 6) or

79

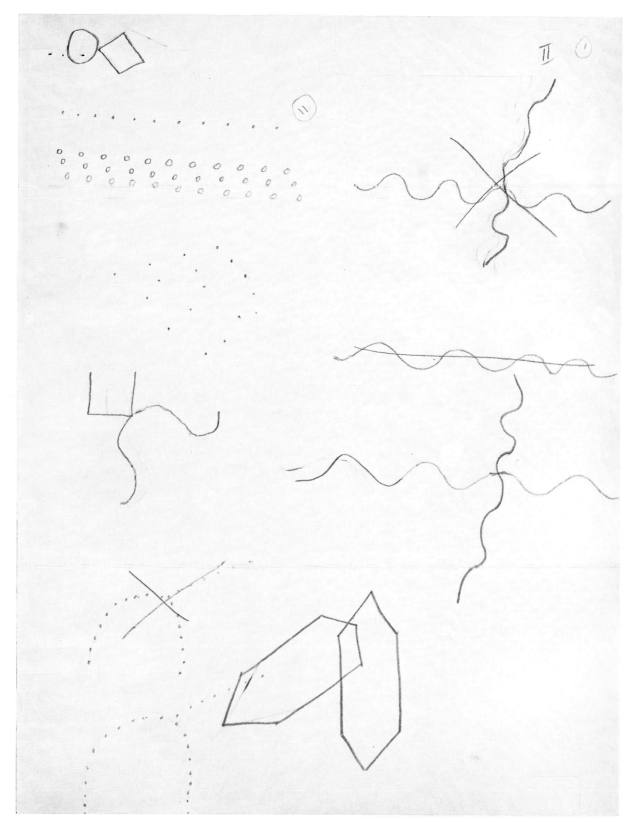

Figure 50a.

Figure 50b.

Figure 51.

the control of aggressivity may be reflected in the blunted or curved arrow demonstrating anxiety over its free expression (Fig. 18) or in subtle exaggerations of all angles, or recurring penetrations which suggest that a sadistic quality pervades all interactions.

Gender conflict may permeate the series as in Figure 17, which as previously noted is drawn by a woman who is so conflicted about the feminine that on her recall the lines of spaced circles are replaced by lines of squares, the breast on Bender Figure 4 is phallicized, and the huge misshapen feminine circle of Bender Card A totally dominates the pathetic masculine square.

A more dramatic and specific problem is expressed in Figures 52a and b (copy and recall) by a female candidate for a transsexual operation who first alters Bender Card 7 in the *copy* (always ominous) by notching the phallic extension, and then in the recall proceeds to notch all similar pointed extensions. Here the obsessive preoccupation with the absence of a phallus—true concrete penis envy—dominates the performance. The push of anxiety to achieve the male genitalia, her sense of deprivation and disfigurement in the body of a woman becomes the central theme, and though confirmed in the other projectives, is certainly clearly indicated, from the beginning, in the Bender.

Besides the thematic and stylistic significance of repeated distortions, a rich field for exploration is provided by the endless contaminations —that is figures produced on the Recall that combine elements of two of the figures originally presented to copy. These combinations have the significance of contaminations on the Rorschach: they reflect a serious disturbance in psychic functioning, loss of boundaries, an inability to keep separate what is in reality separate, to maintain the integrity of the memory trace of an experience. The degree of cognitive disruption reflected by these new figures suggests a psychotic level of pathology.

The particular fusions are important. What are the elements that go into the new combined figure? What confluence of different spheres, or needs, aspects, qualities does the fusion imply? In Figure 11 we note a simple distortion in Bender Cards A and 4 (reflecting the masculine-feminine relationships) and recognize this to be an area of tension. On Figure 12, the recall, this is confirmed. One figure combines a part of Card A and Card 4, or Card 4 and Card 5. The circle seems to be rising up through the floor of the square. Certainly this person has difficulty in sorting out a viable gender identity, and is threatened by the passive feminine aspect which is experienced as intruding on and threatening to eclipse his masculine integrity.

These fused patterns, gross and subtle, begin to stand out as one works with the Bender. What is roughly sketched out by initial clues provided by this easily administered and fascinating test becomes

Figure 52a.

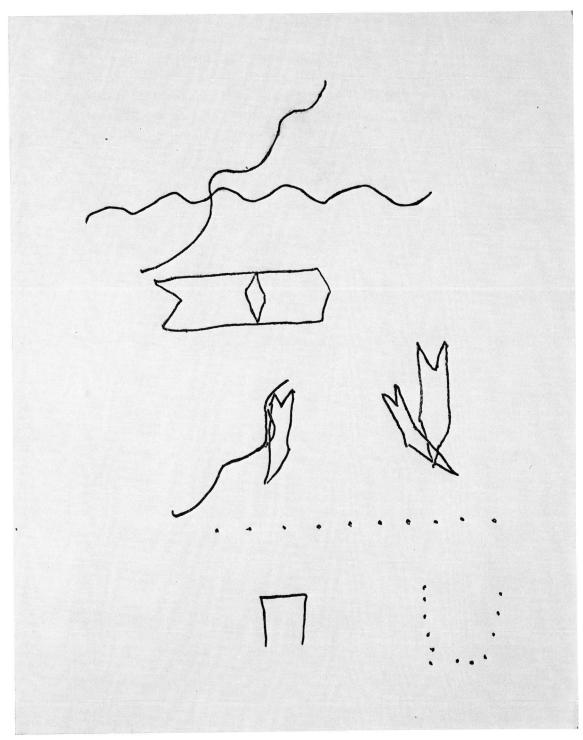

Figure 52b.

confirmed, modified, or subtly or sharply shifted by material from other projectives. To my mind, the Bender is best used projectively as the initial test in a battery to alert us to what will be confirmed, amplified or changed later on. Experienced examiners will have the satisfaction of spotting dramatic correlations, of sudden and sometimes surprisingly accurate insights. But symbols which are this reductive must always be recognized as bearing potentially multiple meanings, and though we may speak with some confidence on generalities, the specific, elaborated significance should be tentative, awaiting the corroboration of other material.